THE YOUNG WOMAN'S GUIDE

by

William A. Alcott

ISBN-13:
978-1979661836

ISBN-10:
1979661839

PREFACE.

This work was begun, soon after the appearance of the Young Man's Guide—and was partially announced to the public. For reasons, however, which I have not room to give in this place, it was thought proper to defer its publication till the appearance of several other volumes in the same spirit, involving more particularly the relative duties.

I wish to have it distinctly understood, that I do not propose to give a complete manual of the social and moral duties of young women. Every one has his own way of looking at things, and I have mine. Some of the duties of young women have appeared to me to receive from other writers less attention than their comparative importance demands; and others—especially those which are connected with the great subject of "temperance in all things"—I have believed to be treated, in several respects, erroneously.

Permit me, however, to say, that while I have not intended to follow the path, or repeat the ideas of any other writer, I have not attempted to avoid either the one or the other. If I have presented here and there a thought which had already come before the public from my own pen, I can only say that I did not intend it, although I did not take special pains to avoid it. The sum is this. I have presented my thoughts, without so much reference to what has already been said by myself or others, as to what I have supposed to be the necessities of those for whom I write. I have gone straight forward, asking no questions; and I trust I shall be dealt with in a manner equally direct.

CONTENTS.

CHAPTER XXXI. SOCIAL IMPROVEMENT.

CHAPTER XXXII. MORAL PROGRESS.

THE YOUNG WOMAN'S GUIDE

CHAPTER I.

EXPLANATION OF TERMS.

Defining terms. The word excellence here used as nearly synonym with holiness. What is meant by calling the work a Guide. The term Woman—why preferable, as a general term, to Lady. The class to whom this work is best adapted.

It has been said, and with no little truth, that a large proportion of the disputes in the world might have been avoided, had the disputants first settled the meaning of the terms they respectively used. In like manner might a large share of the misapprehension and error in the world be avoided, if those who attempt to teach, would first explain their terms.

This work is called "The Young Woman's Guide to EXCELLENCE," because it is believed that excellence, rather than happiness, should be the leading aim of every human being. I am not ignorant that happiness—present and future—is proposed as our "being's end and aim," not only by as distinguished a poet as Alexander Pope, but also by as distinguished a philosopher as William Paley. But these men did not learn in the school of Christ, that our "beings end and aim" is happiness, present or future. The Christian religion, no less than Christian philosophy and sound common sense, teaches that holiness or excellence should be the leading aim of mankind. Not that "the recompense of reward," to which the best men of the world have had regard in all their conduct, is to be wholly overlooked, but only that it should not be too prominent in the mind's eye, and too exclusively the soul's aim; since it would thus be but a more refined and more elevated selfishness. Real excellence brings happiness along with it. Like godliness—which, indeed, is the same thing—it has the promise of the life that now is, and of that which is to come. And that happiness which is attainable without personal excellence or holiness, is either undeserved or spurious. The world. I know, very generally seek after it, whether deserved or undeserved; and whether willing or not to pay the price.

My object is to assist, if I can, in removing from our world the error of seeking happiness as a primary object. Let us but pursue excellence, and happiness will almost inevitably follow. I address this exhortation to Young Women, in particular, for reasons which will be seen when I come, in the next chapter, to speak of female responsibilities. Let every young woman aspire to high degrees of purity and excellence. Let her great aim be, to be personally holy—like God her Saviour. To this end and with this aim, let her be ready to set aside, if necessary, father and mother, and brother and sister—yes, and her own life also,—assured that if she does it with a sacred regard to God and duty, all will be well. Let her but follow Christ according to the gospel plan, if it lead her to prison and to death. But it will not thus lead her. For every self-denial or self-sacrifice it involves, she will secure, as a general rule, manifold more in this present life, and in the world to come, life everlasting.

This book is not called "The Young Woman's GUIDE," with the expectation that she will consider it her only or even her principal guide. The Bible should be the principal guide of every person, young or old, male or female. Parents, also, are invaluable as guides. I offer it only as the best guide which my reflections upon those subjects, connected with the welfare of young women, that come within the department of my study and observation, enable me to give. May it prove a guide indeed!

I have called it "The Young WOMAN'S Guide," because there are many who are accustomed to associate with the word lady; the idea of exemption from labor, and of entire devotion to something supposed to be above it—as fashionable company, or fashionable dress and equipage. And not a few can hardly hear the word mentioned without disgust. Miss Sedgwick has illustrated this part of my subject very happily in the first and fifteenth chapters of her "Means and Ends." She says she does not write exclusively for those who are termed young *ladies;* because she does not believe in any such fixed class, in the country. The term *lady*, she also says, is too indefinite for any valuable use. We not only apply it to those who are, or would be, above labor, but in a great many other ways—as that "old lady," meaning, perhaps, some beggar at the door, &c.

In short, she does not like the use of the phrase, young lady, at all. Neither do I. Besides, I like best the good old fashioned term, YOUNG WOMAN. This exactly represents the class for whom I write, and that, too, without either explanation or qualification. It will be mistaken by no one, nor will it be likely to give or cause any offence.

Finally, I call the work "The YOUNG Woman's Guide," because I design it for those single persons of the female sex to whom the term young is usually applied; viz., those who are from twelve or fourteen to eighteen or twenty years of age—and to those, in general, who are single. I hope, nevertheless, that it will contain some thoughts which may be useful to those individuals who are in married life, as well as to those who are below the age of twelve years. Many of its suggestions and principles will, indeed, be applicable—so far as they are just or true—to all mankind.

CHAPTER II.

FEMALE RESPONSIBILITIES.

Comparison of the responsibilities of young men and young women. Saying of Dr. Rush. Its application to young women. Definition of the term education. Bad and good education. Opinions of Solomon. Influence of a young woman in a family—in a school. Anecdotes of female influence. West, Alexander, Cæsar, Franklin. Story of a domestic in Boston. The good she is doing. Special influence of young women in families—and as sisters. Female influence in the renovation of the world.

Much has been said, within a few years, of the duties, responsibilities, &c., of young men, especially the young men of our republic. A great deal that has been said, has, in my view, been appropriate and well-timed. My own attention has been frequently turned to the same class of individuals; nor do I regret it. My only regret is, that what I have said, has not been said to better purpose. Counsels and cautions to young men, standing on slippery places as they confessedly do, can hardly be too numerous, provided those who give them, use discretion, and remember their responsibility, not only to the tribunal of public opinion, but to a tribunal still higher.

The snares, the dangers, the difficulties, the influence, the responsibilities of young men—at least in the United States—can hardly be overrated. Would that they could be so trained and directed as fully to understand them, and govern themselves accordingly! Would that they could be made to exert that moral influence in the salvation of our race—politically no less than morally, nationally no less than individually—of which they are so capable.

Yet, after every concession of this kind, I am compelled to believe that the responsibilities and influence of young women—to say nothing at present of their dangers—are much more weighty than those of young men. I am decidedly of opinion, that the future holiness and happiness of the world in which we live, depend much more on the character of the rising generation of the female sex, than on the character of our young men.

It was said by Dr. Rush, long ago, that mothers and school-masters plant the seeds of nearly all the good and evil in our world.

Presuming that by school-masters he meant teachers of both sexes, will any one doubt the truth of his assertion? Will any one doubt the justness of a remark in the late "Western Review," that if this world is ever to become a better and a happier world, woman must be foremost, if not the principal agent in rendering it so?

But as mothers are never mothers till they have been daughters, is it not obvious that the right education of these last is as great a work as any to which human mind and human effort have ever been called? If woman moves the world, intellectually, morally, and even, in effect, politically—as no doubt she does—is it not of primary importance that she be taught, as well as teach herself, to move it right?

Can it be necessary to advert, in this place, to the well known and acknowledged fact, that almost every man of extensive influence, for good or for evil, whom the world has produced, became what he was through maternal influence? Cæsar, and Caligula, and Talleyrand, and Napoleon, became what they were in consequence of their mothers, no less than Alfred, and Doddridge, and Howard, and Washington. For let it not be forgotten that mothers and teachers, according to Dr. Rush—and, in fact, according to common observation, too—plant the seeds of the world of evil no less than of the world of good. How exceedingly important, then, that *they* should be well educated, "from whom," in the language of another writer, "our virtues are, and from whom our vices may be"—we would add *must* be—"derived;" at least in no small proportion!

But I am using the term education without explaining it. Let me, then, ere I proceed to say more on the subject of female responsibility, explain what I mean by education, especially female education.

Mere instruction in the sciences is, indeed, education; it is, however, but a very small part of it. To educate, is to train up. In this view, all are of course educated; and every thing which has an influence in developing mind or body, and in training up, either for good or for evil, is entitled, justly, to the name of education.

But if the above definition be just—if whatever concerns our development, or the formation of any part of our character, physical, intellectual, social or moral, is education—then it must follow that there are two kinds of education, bad and good. All persons, places and things, which affect us (and what does not affect us?) and influence us, for good or for evil, must educate us.

I am aware that this definition is not new: still, it is not generally received, or if received, not generally acted upon. There is still an almost universal clinging to the old, inadequate, incorrect idea, that the principal part of education consists in the cultivation of the intellect; and that, too, by set lessons; received, for the most part, at the schools. The true idea of education, therefore, must be continually enforced, till it becomes common property, and until mankind act as if they believed what they profess in regard to it.

When Solomon says, "Train up a child in the way he should go," he is talking of what I call *education;* and the kind of education which he is there recommending, is *good* education. I do not believe he had the schools in his mind—the infant school, the Sabbath school, the common school, the high school, or the university.

Far be it from me to attempt to detract from the value of our schools; on the contrary, I regard them as of inestimable worth, when duly attended to. What I insist on is, that they are not the *all in all* of education; and that, in fact, their influence in training up or forming good character, is so trifling—that is, comparatively—that they scarcely deserve to be thought of when speaking of education, as a whole, especially the education of daughters. And though one of the tribes of the nation to which Solomon belonged, over which he reigned, and for whom, in particular, he wrote, is said to have been school-masters by profession, and another priests, I can hardly conceive that when he was inspired to give the educational advice just alluded to, he ever turned so much as a thought to the little corner of Palestine allotted to Simeon, or to the Levites in their respective but more scattered stations.

Solomon was, in all probability, addressing himself chiefly to the fathers and mothers, and grand-fathers and grand-mothers, and other relatives of Israel; the class who, by their united influence, make the son and daughter, and grand-son and grand-daughter, what they are—a blessing or a curse to the world in which they are to live. For, according as children are brought up by these teachers, and by the influences which are shed upon them from day to day and from hour to hour, so are they well or ill educated.

If I have been successful in presenting the meaning of a term which is not only frequently used in this book, but almost every where else, it will follow, as a matter of course, that I do not attach too much importance to the education of daughters themselves, nor to their education as the teachers of others. For if to educate, is to form character, what young woman can be found, of any age or in any family, who is not a teacher?

Have young women often considered—daughters, especially—how much they influence younger brothers and sisters, if any such there are in the family where they dwell? Have they considered how much they sometimes influence the character—and how much more they might do it—not only of their school-mates and play-mates, but also of their more aged friends and companions—their parents, grand-parents, and others? [Footnote: On reading these paragraphs in manuscript, to one of our more eminent teachers, he observed that if he had been useful in the world, he owed his usefulness to the exertions of a maiden lady who resided in his father's family, while his character was forming.]

I could tell them—were this the place for it—many a true story of reading daughters who have been the means of awakening, in their aged parents, or grand-parents, or other friends, a taste for reading, which they might otherwise have gone down to the grave without acquiring. I could tell them of many a father and mother, and grand-father and grand-mother, grown grey in vice—hardened even by intemperance as well as other vices—who have been reformed by the prattle, or the reproof, or the prayers of a good daughter. Is not such a daughter a teacher?

But I am most anxious to convince young women of their responsibilities in regard to the rising generation, especially their own brothers and companions. I am anxious, if I can, to convince all who read this volume, that God has, by his providence, committed to their charge, in no small degree, the bodies, and minds, and the souls of those with whom, in this world, they are associated. That according to their own conduct, good or ill, will be, in no small measure, the health, and knowledge, and excellence of their friends and companions. That according to their efforts—attended, either by the blessing of God, or the tokens of his displeasure—will be the condition of millions, for time and for eternity.

But is it so? Are daughters, as daughters merely—to say nothing, as yet, of maternal influence—are daughters thus influential? Is it true that the destiny of millions is thus committed to their keeping?

I have seen the conduct of a whole school—I speak now of the common or district school—graduated by the conduct of a single virtuous, and amiable, and intelligent young woman, not twelve years old, who attended it. I have seen a whole Sabbath school not a little affected by the prompt attention, decorous behaviour and pious example of some elder member of an older class, to whom the younger members of classes, male and female, looked up, as to a sort of monitor, or I know not what to call it—for the impression thus made, is better seen and felt than described. The bad behaviour of a young woman, in these circumstances, is, indeed, equally influential—nay, more so, inasmuch as the current of human nature sets more readily downward than upward. Still, a good example is influential—greatly so: would that it were generally known how much so!

Suppose now that by your good behaviour and pious example in the Sabbath school, you are the means of turning the attention of one younger companion, male or female, to serious things, and of bringing down upon that young person the blessing of Almighty God. Suppose that individual should live to teach or to preach, or in some other form to bless the world, by bringing numbers to the knowledge, and love, and inculcation of the very truth which has saved his own soul—and these last, in their turn, should become apostles or missionaries to others, and so on. Is there any end, at least till the world comes to an end, of the good influence which a good Sabbath school pupil *may* thus exert?

But this is something more than a supposed case. Is it not, in effect, just what is actually taking place around us in the world continually? Not, indeed, that a long train of good influences has been frequently set agoing in the Sabbath school—for Sabbath schools are but of recent origin. But people have always been led along to virtue or vice, to piety or impiety, to bless the world or to prove a curse to it, by one another. A word or a look from a relative, or friend, or acquaintance, in the school or somewhere else, has often given a turn to the whole character. A word, it is said, may move a continent. Something less than a word—a look or a smile of approbation—may move more than a continent. It may move not merely a West, [Footnote: A mother's kiss, in token of her approbation of some little pencil sketch, is believed by Benjamin West to have given the turn to his character—the character of a who said, and justly, that he painted for eternity. "That mother's kiss," he observes, "made me a painter."] but an Alexander, a Cæsar, a Napoleon, a Washington and a Howard—men who, in their turn, moved a world!

I have spoken of the influence which a young woman may have on millions through the medium of the Sabbath school. But if she may influence in this way, the millions of those who are to come after her, how much more may she do in forming character for the great future, in the family! Her presence in the Sabbath school is only once a week—an hour or two a day, once in seven days; whereas, her influence in the family is going on perpetually.

The clothes of Alexander the Great, are said to have been made, to a very great extent, by his sisters; and those of Augustus Cæsar were made for many years, by his. And can we doubt that these young females were influential, in a great many respects, in the education of these conquerors? What could the latter have done, but for the assistance and influence of mothers and sisters? And can we have any Alexanders and Cæsars, at the present day, to carry on the moral and intellectual conquests which are so necessary in the world, without the aid and co-operation of mothers and sisters?

Sisters little know—it is almost impossible for them ever to know—how much they do to bring about results,—to educate their brothers and friends, for the work which they perform, whether good or evil. The sisters of Franklin little knew what they were doing for "young Benny," as they called him, while they assisted their mother in taking care of his clothes, in preparing his food, and in ministering to his other physical wants—yes, and to the wants of his mind, too. Who can say that Benjamin Franklin would ever have been what Benjamin Franklin was, without their aid, joined to the efforts of their mother?

Many a young female, having caught, in some degree, the spirit of doing good, has sighed for opportunities. "What can I do?" she has seemed to say, "here at home. If I could be a missionary at Ceylon, or South Africa, or the Sandwich Islands, or even if I could be a teacher, I could, perhaps, do something. But as it is, I must remain a mere cypher in the world. I would do good, but I have no opportunities."

She who says this, is undoubtedly sincere. She is, however, greatly mistaken. Her opportunities for doing good—for exerting an influence to bless her race—"are neither few nor small." There is, indeed, a difference, a very great difference, in human conditions and circumstances; and yet I am persuaded, no female is so secluded as not to be able to fulfil, towards her race, a most important mission.

I know of an excellent female who is often heard lamenting her want of opportunity for usefulness. She has the spirit of doing good as she supposes, and as I fully believe. And yet she is miserable—she makes herself so—by repining continually at her want of ability to perform the good works which her heart meditates. She would rejoice to devote her self to the elevation of her race. She would gladly go to India, or the South Seas, if her age and uncultivated intellect did not exclude her from being a candidate. Now, without saying a word in disparagement of foreign missions—for the success of which I would gladly contribute largely, not only by prayers, but by pecuniary contributions—truth compels me to say of this female, that I am by no means sure she could do more for humanity, or more, in fact, for the cause of Christ, by a foreign mission, than she is now doing by a domestic one.

A *domestic* mission hers indeed is, in the fullest sense of the term. She is an ordinary domestic—and no more—in the family to which she belongs. But what is the condition of that family? The head of it is the distinguished teacher of a private female seminary. Here he has prepared hundreds of young women—so far, I mean, as the mere instruction of what he calls a "family school," is concerned—for usefulness as teachers, as sisters, as ministers to the aged, and as mothers to the young. Suppose he has instructed, in his comparatively excellent way, two hundred females. Suppose again one half of the females he has instructed and counselled and lived among, should, in their turn, each form as much character as he has already done—and he is yet but a middle aged man; and suppose half the disciples of each of these pupils in their turn should do the same, and thus on, till the year of our Lord 2000, only, which is, as we have reason to believe, but a little way towards the end of the world. Suppose one hundred only of each two hundred, should live to have influence, seventy-five of them as the mothers of families of the usual size, and twenty-five only, as teachers. There will then be five generations in one hundred and sixty years; and the number of children which will come under the influence of this line or succession of mothers and teachers, will be no less than ninety millions; or a number equal to six times the present population of the United States.

Now what I have here supposed, is by no means beyond the pale of possibility. Two hundred pupils is not a large number for one teacher to instruct during his whole life. Nor is twenty-five a large proportion of two hundred to become teachers. Nor is seventy-five a large number in two hundred to live to have families; nor two children in each family, upon an average, a very large number to come to maturity and have families in their turn. Besides, I have reckoned but four generations in one hundred and sixty years, exclusive of that now educating. So that I have kept my estimates within due bounds in every respect.

Do you ask what the domestic of whom I have spoken has to do with all this? I answer, much—very much indeed. Has she not rendered to the teacher in whose employ she has been, that kind of services, without which he could not have followed his occupation? And if ninety millions, or even one tenth that number of citizens should, in the course of the next two centuries, reap the benefit of his labors, and become lights in the world, is it too much to say that she has been an important aid in accomplishing the work? Nay, is it even too much to affirm that unless the part which she has acted had been performed by her or somebody else, the school could not have gone on, and two hundred young women could not have received the teacher's instructions?

Why, then, is not this humble domestic to whom I allude, a benefactor to her race—if a benefaction it is, to raise up and qualify for usefulness two hundred females—as well as he who has the whole credit of it? I will not, indeed, say that any thing like as much credit is due to her as to him; but I may say, and with truth, that she was an important auxiliary in producing the results that have been mentioned.

But if a humble domestic, one who imagines herself so obscure as to be of little service to a world which perhaps estimates her services almost as low as she does herself—if such an individual may, besides the general influence of her character upon a family, be an indispensable aid in the work of sending forth to the world a host of female missionaries, equal, in the progress of less than two centuries, at the dawn of the millennium, to ninety millions, what may not be done by a sister in *a well ordered family*—one who is not only well educated and governed herself, but who educates and governs others well?

It may indeed be said, that a domestic, in the family of a distinguished teacher, may indirectly influence, by her labors in the way I have mentioned, a far greater number of her race than most sisters are able to do. It may, indeed, be so. There is, however, another consideration. It is chiefly the externals of education which can receive attention, even in our best private schools. Little can be done, at the best, to form character—deep, permanent, and abiding character. Blessings indeed—great blessings—such schools are; but in proportion as their numbers are increased beyond those of our larger families, in the same proportion is the influence which might be exerted by the teacher, scattered and weakened; whereas, if the number be small, the influence of those who teach by example and by precept, is concentrated, and rendered efficient. There is no certainty that the feebler influence which is exerted on ninety millions, might not do more good by being concentrated on one tenth or one twentieth that number. In other words, if the same amount of pains were taken by mothers and sisters, and the same amount of labor bestowed for the purpose, there is no certainty that the world might not as soon be rendered what it should be through the medium of family education alone, as with the aid of other influences. Christianity, when brought to bear upon the family by the united exertions of father, mother, brothers and sisters, will probably have an influence on the regeneration of the world, of which no human mind—uninspired at least—has ever yet conceived.

Would that our young females—sisters especially—had but an imperfect conception of the power they possess to labor in the cause of human improvement! Would that they had but an imperfect idea of female responsibility!

My remarks are applicable to all young women; but they are particularly so to elder sisters. To them is given in special charge, the happiness and the destiny of all younger brothers and sisters, be they ever so numerous. As the desires of Abel were to be expressed to Cain, and the latter was appointed to rule over the former, so is the elder daughter appointed to rule over those whom God has, in the same manner, committed to her trust. Happy is she who has right views of her weighty responsibilities; but thrice happy is she who not only understands her duty, but does it!

But if the moral character, much more than the physical and intellectual well being of the family, is given in charge to elder sisters, and even to all sisters, it is scarcely possible for them to form a correct idea of the weight of their influence, in this respect at least, till they are past the age when that influence is most necessary, most persuasive, and most effectual.

I have seldom found a young man who had strayed long and widely from the path of virtue, who had enjoyed the society and influence of a wise, and virtuous, and attentive sister. On the contrary, I have almost uniformly found such individuals to have been in families where there were no sisters, or where the sisters were not what they ought to have been; or to have been kept at schools where there were none but our sex.

I beseech every young female reader to make herself acquainted, as far as she possibly can, with the nature of her influence, and the consequent responsibilities which devolve upon her. Let her understand that the day has gone by in which physical force was supposed to rule the world. Moral influence is now the order of the day; and they whose moral influence is most weighty and powerful, are they who most effectually bear rule. But as it is reserved for woman, when sensible, enlightened, virtuous and pious, to exercise the most weighty moral influence, consequently it is her province most effectually to bear rule. Kings, and emperors, and presidents, parliaments, and congresses, and assemblies, and courts, and legislators, and judges, may labor in vain to influence or to reform mankind, so long as female influence is not what it should be. But let females be rightly educated, and let them do what a good education will enable them to do, and vice will ere long hang her head, and virtue and piety—which alone exalt a nation, or the individuals that compose it—will resume their sway. Then will the wilderness and the solitary place be glad, and the desert rejoice and blossom as the rose.

CHAPTER III.

SELF-EDUCATION.

Views of Agesilaus, king of Sparta—of Solomon, king of Israel. Mistake corrected. What the wisest and best parents cannot do. What, therefore, remains to the daughter. Necessity of self-education. The work of self-education the work of life—a never-ending progress upward to the throne of God.

Woman, then, now so often miseducated, must be trained in the way she should go. But let us consider a little more in detail what this education or training of woman should be, and what it should accomplish.

When Agesilaus, king of Sparta, was asked what things he thought most proper for boys to learn, he replied—"Those which they ought to practise when they come to be men." Nor does this essentially differ from the direction of Solomon, which has been quoted.

If females do, in effect, rule the world, they ought, as I have before said, to be trained to sway the sceptre of moral rule in the right manner. If they now stand in the same position, as regards the world and the world's happiness, with that which boys were supposed to occupy in the days of Agesilaus, and if this thing was correct in his opinion, then it follows that a proper answer to the question, What things are most proper for girls to learn? would be—Those which they ought to practise when they come to be women.

But it will not be forgotten that the definition I have given of the term education includes much more than merely direct efforts to teach. Whatever affects the health or the progress of body, mind or soul, even though it were that in which the individual is mostly passive, as in sleep, is a part of our education.

There is one point in which the views of Agesilaus concerning education, if not incorrect, are at least defective. He appears to countenance an idea, still very prevalent, that children and youth are not only in a state of preparation for the future, but a state of preparation, *merely*.

They are to be taught what they ought to practise when they come to be men, according to Agesilaus; but according to the views of one who was wiser than he, they are to be trained in the way they should go. The latter view comes nearer the truth of the case than the former. It requires, or at least permits us, to train up the child to-day for the enjoyments of to-day, as well as for those of to-morrow—a point which the maxim of Agesilaus does not seem to include.

Young people are taught, almost universally—by example, if not by precept—to consider merit, if not virtue and happiness, as belonging exclusively to maturity. They are not enough assured that youth, though a state of preparation and trial, is also a state of reward; and that neither usefulness nor happiness is confined to place, age or circumstances.

I wish to see the day arrive when the young—young women, especially—will not look forward so much to a distant day and to distant circumstances, for a theatre of action, and for the rewards of action, as they are accustomed to do; for they thus deprive themselves of a vast amount of happiness which is due them in the *present*, without in the least enhancing the value or the pleasures of the future.

I wish to see them so educated that they will not only be what they should be, when they come to adult age, but also what they should be now. They have or should have a character to acquire *now*; a reputation to secure and maintain *now*; and a sphere of personal usefulness and happiness to occupy *now*.

It is true, indeed, that childhood and youth are more specially seasons of preparation, and less specially seasons of reward, than maturer and later life; but it is also equally true, that every stage of life, not excepting its very evening, is little more than a preparation for a still higher state, where reward will predominate in a degree which will make all previous preparation seem to dwindle almost to nothing.

Existence, in short, is a state of progress, having, at every step, so far as we know, its trials and rewards— the rewards always, however, predominating, and the trials diminishing, in proportion as personal holiness renders the latter unnecessary.

It will happen, unavoidably, that many young women to whom this little volume may come, will have been trained up, to the time of casting their eyes on these pages, in the old fashioned belief to which I have alluded—viz., that they can neither *do* nor *be* much in the world, except to submit passively to certain processes which have received the name of education, till their arrival at a certain size or age. The fault, reader—if such should be the case—is not chargeable, solely, on your parents. They followed a custom which they found; they did not make it. But however this may be, it is clear that your great object should now be, to see what you can do for yourself.

Now, then, here you are, twelve, fourteen, perhaps sixteen years of age. Your parents have brought you up according to the existing customs, *for the future*. They have not sought to make you feel your present responsibilities, your present power to do good, your present capacity for communicating and securing happiness, so much as to make you believe there are responsibilities, and powers, and capacities, and rewards, to be yours when you come to be large enough and old enough to appreciate or receive them.

But whatever your parents may have left undone in regard to the formation of your character, it is yours to do. Need I urge the necessity of the case? The present is an exceedingly important period of your life; and what is to be done, must be done quickly. But what your parents have hitherto left undone, they will be likely to continue to leave undone. Unless you apply yourself, therefore—and that immediately—to the finishing of a work, that, owing to the circumstances in which they have been and still are placed, and the views they have entertained, they have left unfinished, your education is not likely to be, by any means, so perfect as it should be. You must take it up, therefore, where they have left it; and do, for yourself, what they have not done for you. In other words, you must engage, at once, in the great work of self-education.

It may, indeed, be the case, that you are the child of parents who have done their best, and who have done it intelligently. Blessed is the young woman who has such parents, but thrice blessed are the parents themselves, if, in the performance of their work, they have the co-operation of the daughter. There must be self-education even where there are the best of parents. In fact, the work of parental training and that of self-education, should go on together; they cannot well be separated. Parental effort will produce but half its legitimate results, when not seconded by the efforts of infancy and childhood, and especially of youth. The reasons for this are so obvious that they hardly need to be repeated. No young woman can be constantly in the company of her mother; no mother can constantly watch over her daughter. In the best families there are hours of each day, when the child of every age, especially of youthful age and capacity, must be left to herself or to the influence of others. What, then, is to become of her? Is she to yield to that current of the world which every where sets downward?

You will say, perhaps, that she has good habit on her side, together with the counsels of good and kind parents. If so, I say again, she is highly favored. But what if it happen to be otherwise? What if the parents happen not to be wise and discriminating, or seem unable to find time, in the bustle of a busy world, to do that which they know it were desirable to do? What then?

I repeat the sentiment, then: if you have the best of parents, you are liable, at your age, to be thrown, day after day, into new and untried circumstances—such as it were next to impossible for parents to foresee. New feelings will arise unknown to yourself, and undiscoverable by them. New passions will make their appearance—new temptations will solicit—new trials will be allotted you, In spite of the best parental efforts at education, there will still remain to you a great work of *self*-effort.

To assist you in it, is the leading object of this little volume. It is not a substitute for parental counsels. It is not a substitute for your own reflections. If it prove not an aid to parents, in their task, and if it encourage not the reflection and the self-efforts of the young, it will not accomplish its object.

In the preceding chapter I have endeavored to give a general idea of education, as I understand and use the term. In this I have shown that no small part of the great work of education devolves, in the best circumstances—and much more in circumstances which are unfavorable—upon the daughter. I have shown that her whole life is a state of preparation, indeed—but also, in some measure, a state of reward.

You perceive your own character and happiness, for time and for eternity, to be placed, in no small degree and measure, in your own hands—the efforts of parents, friends and teachers to the contrary notwithstanding. You perceive the formation of that character, by the combined efforts of your parents and others and yourself, to constitute the work of your education. You perceive yourself capable—at least I hope you do—of everlasting progress; of approaching the great source of Light, and Truth, and Knowledge, and Excellence, forever and ever, though without the possibility of attaining it. You perceive that, though allied on the one side to the dust you tread on, you are allied on the other side to heaven; that though connected by ties of consanguinity to the worm you are also connected, or may be, with angels and archangels, and cherubim and seraphim, in the glorious work of unceasing progress upward toward the throne of God. Will you not, then, hail with joy, every effort of every being who would assist your spirit in its upward flight?

To educate yourself—to make progress—to ascend toward the Eternal Throne,—you must know yourself—the laws within and without you—your relations, by means of those laws, to other things and other beings—your powers, your capacities, your prerogatives. You must, moreover, know how to govern yourself in accordance with your knowledge.

CHAPTER IV

LOVE OF IMPROVEMENT.

Female capabilities. Doing every thing in the best possible manner. Unending progress. Every person and every occupation susceptible of improvement, indefinitely. Doing well what is before us. Anecdote illustrative of this principle. Personal duties. Two great classes of persons described. Hopes of reaching the ears of the selfish.

I have already said that you are capable of never-ending progress in knowledge and excellence, and that it is alike your interest and your duty to aspire to that perfection for which God has given you capabilities. The object of the present chapter is to kindle within you a desire to make progress in every thing you do—to go on, as the Scripture expresses it, to perfection.

"Whatever is worth doing, is worth doing well," is an old but true maxim. More than even this might be affirmed. Whatever is worth doing at all, is worth doing in the best possible manner. No matter how well you have done the same thing heretofore; no matter how much more perfectly you already do it than your neighbors. You are not to make the past of your own experience, or the present of your neighbor's, the measure of your conduct. The question is—How well can I perform this particular act now?

Perhaps no person who reads these paragraphs, will doubt the truth of the general principle I have laid down. Thus far, it may be said, all seems to be correct. We are, indeed, bound to do every thing we do, to the glory of God; and he can hardly be glorified in the doing of a thing in a manner which is short of the best in our power.

Yet, when we come to apply the principle, and say in what particulars we should strive to make progress and do better, from day to day, and from hour to hour, (if the thing is to be performed so often,) many an individual will be found, I fear, to stand back; and among those who thus shrink from the just application of admitted principle, will be found not a few who, till now, supposed they had within them a strong desire for perpetual improvement.

It is, my young friends, no *trifling* matter to have burning within a hearty desire for eternal progress. It is no small thing to do whatever our hands find to do, which it is fit that an intelligent being—one who belongs to the family of Christ—*should* do, in such a manner that it will contribute to the glory of God, and the good of mankind.

And yet less than this, as Christians or even as rational and immortal beings, we cannot do. I know, indeed, that many who profess to be the disciples of Christ, actually do less than this. I know there are hundreds and thousands who are called by his worthy name, and who seem to be almost above the liability to do that which could be regarded as positively wrong, who, nevertheless, are very far from striving to do everything which their hands find to do *with all their might*—or, in other words, as well as they possibly can. But it is to be hoped that the standard of Christian character will ere long be much higher than it is now.

It is of far less consequence *what* we do in the world, my young friends, than how well we do it. There is hardly a useful occupation among us, in which a person may not be eminently serviceable to himself and to mankind. There is hardly one in which we may not constantly improve ourselves. There is hardly one which will not afford us the means and opportunities of improving others. There is hardly an occupation which may not itself be essentially improved.

I do not mean to say there is no choice in occupations, either as regards pleasantness or usefulness. Nor do I mean to say, that neither parents themselves nor their children, are ever to consult their own natural preferences—their own likes and dislikes. All I aim at is, to convince the young—especially the young woman—that the old couplet,

> "Honor and shame from no condition rise;
> Act well your part, there all the honor lies"—

is not so very far from the truth, as many suppose; and that happiness, and even usefulness and excellence, are as little dependent on place and condition, as honor and shame.

A mercantile man with whom I was once acquainted, gave me, in few words, a very important lesson. He said he made it the rule of his life to do, in the best possible manner, whatever at any time seemed, as a subject of duty, to devolve upon him. No matter about his own likes or dislikes—what appeared to be in the course of the dispensations of Providence allotted him for the day, he performed with all his heart. If he should conclude to pursue his present business for life, as the means of procuring a livelihood, this would be the very best course of preparation: if otherwise, it was the best under the circumstances; and especially was it the best state of mental and moral discipline with which he could be furnished.

To neglect the business before us because we are unhappy in it, or at least not so happy as we fancy we might be in some other employment, is to oppose the plans of Providence; nay, even to defeat our own purpose. It is to disqualify ourselves, as fast as we can, for faithfulness, and consequently for usefulness, in the employment we desire, should we ever attain to it. The wisest course is, to do what our hands find before them to do, provided it is lawful to do it at all, with all our might.

The best possible preparation a young woman can have for a sphere of action more congenial to her present feelings, is the one she now occupies. She has, at least, duties to herself to perform. Let these, as they recur, be performed in the best possible manner; and let the utmost effort always be made to perform every thing a little better than ever she performed it before—if it be but the washing of a few cups, or the making of a bed. What her personal duties are, generally, need not now be said: first, because many of them are obvious secondly, because they will be treated of in their respective places. But it should ever be borne in mind, that there is nothing ever so trifling, which is worth doing at all, that may not be done better and better at every repetition of the act; and that there is no occupation which may not, in itself, be improved indefinitely.

Rising in the morning, devotion, personal ablutions, dressing, breakfasting, exercise, employments, recreations, dining, conversation, reading, reflection—all these, and a thousand other things which every one, as a general rule, attends to—may be performed in a manner to correspond more and more with the Scripture direction which has been illustrated.

There are, in respect to what I am now mentioning, two classes of persons in the world—of females as well as males; and they differ from each other as widely, almost, as the world of happiness from the world of misery. One of these classes lives to *receive*; is selfish—supremely so. The other lives to *communicate*, more or less—to do good—to make the world around it better. The last class is benevolent.

A person of either class is not necessarily indolent or inactive; but the end and aim of the labors of one, are *herself*; while the other labors for God and mankind. The one procures honey from every flower—formed by other hands—but not a flower does she ever raise by the labor of her own hands, if she can possibly avoid it.

The one lives only to enjoy; the other, to be the continual cause of joy, like her Creator. The latter has a source of happiness within; the former depends for her happiness on others. Leave her alone, or amid a frowning or even an indifferent world, and she is miserable.

Would that I could reach the ears of that numerous class who are dependent on the world around them for their happiness—who never originated any good, and are becoming more and more useless everyday! Would that I could make them believe that true happiness is not to be found externally, unless it first exist in their own bosoms! Would that I could convince them that the royal road to happiness—if there be one—is that which has been alluded to in the preceding paragraphs; in making all persons and things around us better—in transmuting, as it were, under the influence of the gospel, all coarser things around us to "apples of gold in pictures of silver."

I long exceedingly to see our young women filled with the desire of improvement—physical, social, intellectual and moral. I long to see their souls glowing with the desire to go about doing good, like their Lord and Master. Not, indeed, *literally*, as I shall have occasion to say in another place. But I long to have their hearts expand to overflowing with love to the world for whom Christ died; and I wish to have some of the tears of their compassion fall on those over whom God has given them an amazing, and often an unlimited influence.

Could I hope to reach a dozen minds, and warm a dozen hearts, which had otherwise remained congealed, or at most received passively the little stream of happiness which a naked, external world affords them, without any corresponding efforts to form a world of their own—could I be the means of enkindling in them that love for everlasting progress towards perfection, which is so essential to the world's true happiness and their own—could I thus aid in setting in motion an under-current which should, in due time, restore to us Eden, in all its primitive, unfallen beauty and excellence,—how should I be repaid for these labors!

I will dare to hope for the best. If I have the sacred fire burning in my own bosom, I will hope to be the means of enkindling it in the bosom of a few readers. If my own soul glows with love to a fallen world, I will dare to hope that a few, at least, of those whose souls are more particularly made for love and sympathy, will be led to the same source of blessedness.

CHAPTER V.

Vast extent of the science of self-knowledge. Spurious self knowledge. Knowledge of our physical frame—its laws and relations. Examples of the need of this knowledge. Instruments of obtaining it. The use of lectures. Study of our peculiarities. Study of mental philosophy. The Bible. How the Bible should be studied.

Self-knowledge is of the utmost importance to every human being. To no person, however, is it more important than to the young woman.

It is the more necessary to urge the importance of self-knowledge, from the fact that it is a species of knowledge which every one claims, and which she would deem it almost a reflection upon her character to be supposed not to possess; while it is that very knowledge of which almost every one, of both sexes, is exceedingly ignorant.

Such an one "understands himself," is deemed quite a compliment among our sex nor is it wholly disregarded by the other. But by this expression is too often meant no more than a knowledge of the petty acts and shifts, and I might say tricks, by means of which men and women contrive to pass current in the fashionable world. How much this kind of self-acquaintance is worth, is too obvious to need illustration.

I have represented a just self-knowledge as of very great importance; but it is a science of vast extent, as well as of vast importance. A thorough knowledge of one's self includes, first, a knowledge of man in general, in his whole character—compounded as it is—and in all his relations to surrounding beings and things; and, secondly, a knowledge of the peculiarities produced by particular circumstances, condition, mode of life, education and habits.

She who merely understands all the little arts to which I have alluded, which enable us to pass current with a fashionable and grossly wicked world, will find her self-knowledge exceedingly small, when she comes to compare it with the standard of self-acquaintance set up by such writers as Mason, Burgh, Watts, &c.; and, above all, when she comes to compare it with the standard of the Bible. How little, nay, how contemptible will all mere worldly arts and shifts appear—things which at most belong to the department of manners—when she comes to understand her three-fold nature, as exhibited by the natural and revealed laws of Jehovah!

The Subjects of Anatomy, Physiology and Hygiene alone—and they teach us little more than the laws and relations of the mere body or shell of the human being—are almost sufficient for the study of a long life; and yet no individual can ever thoroughly understand herself without them: it is impossible. Anatomy shows us the *structure* of this body, which the Psalmist, long ago, taught us was fearfully and wonderfully made. Physiology teaches us the *laws* by which the living machine operates—is kept in play for seventy, eighty, or a hundred years; and Hygiene teaches us the *relations* of the living, moving human body to surrounding beings and objects. This, indeed, is a knowledge which few young women possess; and yet it is a knowledge which no young woman, who would do her utmost in the work of self-education, can dispense with.

She wishes, perhaps, to improve her voice by conversation, reading and singing. But is she qualified to do this in the best possible manner, while she is wholly ignorant of the structure of the lungs, the wind-pipe, and the fauces, as they are called—parts so intimately concerned in the production of voice and speech?

She wishes, perhaps, to develope and invigorate her muscular system in the highest possible degree; but how can she do this, while she knows almost nothing of the nature or power of the muscular fibre?

She wishes to develope and cultivate her intellectual powers; to acquire "firmness of nerve and energy of thought." But how can she do it, if she is ignorant of the situation and functions of the cerebral and nervous system—that wonderful organ of the intellect?

She would train her eye in the best possible manner; but how can she do so, if she is ignorant of the nature and powers of that wonderful little organ? She would educate, properly, all her senses; but how can she do it, without a knowledge of their structure, functions and relations?

Perhaps she would study the philosophy of dress, and of eating and drinking. How can she do so, till she understands, intimately, the relation of the human system to air, heat, the various kinds of food, drink, &c.?

She would know, still further, the relation of body to mind, and of mind to body—of body and mind to spirit, and of spirit to body and mind. She would study the particular effect of one passion, or faculty, or affection, upon the body, or upon particular functions of the bodily system—and the more remote or more immediate effects of diseases of a bodily organ on mind and spirit. She must know all this, and a thousand times, yea, ten thousand times as much, before she is qualified to go far in the work of self-knowledge.

But she must go beyond even all this, and study her own peculiarities. It is not sufficient to understand the general laws and relations of the human economy; she must understand herself in her own individual character—physically, intellectually and morally. She must understand the peculiarities of her physical frame, of her mental structure, and of her spiritual condition—her relation to other spirits, particularly to the Father of spirits.

How amazing and how extensive—I repeat it—the science of self-knowledge! To be perfect in it we need the life of a Methuselah! But something may be done, even in the short period of seventy years. And if it be but little that we can do in a life time, this consideration only enhances the value of that little.

Something, I have said, may be done in the short period of seventy years. But I might say more. Something may be done in a single day. And years are made up of days. A little done, every day, amounts to much in a whole year.

Let not the individual despair who can get but one new idea respecting herself, in a day. If she can sit down at quiet evening and say, I know something respecting myself which I did not know last night at this time, let her be assured the day is not lost. One idea a day is three hundred and sixty-five a year; and three hundred and sixty-five a year, amount, in seventy years, to twenty-five thousand five hundred and fifty. There *are* those who can hardly be said, at seventy years of age, to have twenty-five thousand five hundred and fifty ideas in their heads.

It is a matter of joy to every friend of self-knowledge, that so many means have been, of late years, devised to facilitate the study of this science. The lectures which have been given to both sexes on the structure, laws and relations of their bodily constitution, and the books which have been written, have made a considerable change in the state of the public sentiment respecting this species of knowledge. For it is not they alone who have heard or read, that have reaped the benefit of hearing and reading on this subject. Many a parent or teacher, aware that such instructions and books were abroad, has been encouraged to the performance of that which she might not have dared to do, had nothing been said or done to encourage her.

Every young woman should, therefore, study these subjects for herself. Such books as those of Miss Sedgwick—her "Poor Rich Man, and Rich Poor Man," and her "Means and Ends"—will prepare the way, or will at least enkindle the desire, for the kind of knowledge of which I am speaking. She will then desire to read the works of the Combes, and perhaps, ere long, some of the other popular books of our day, which treat of Physiology and Hygiene. May I not venture to hope, that at an early stage of her progress, some of the chapters of *this* book will be found serviceable, as well as several other works I have prepared, especially the little volume called the "House I Live In?"

She who, having a hearty desire for improvement in self-knowledge, on an extended scale, lets her years pass without looking into any of the volumes or treatises to which I have referred, can hardly be said to act up to the dignity of a Christian of the nineteenth century.

But it is not the physical department of her nature alone, that she who has the desire for self-knowledge and self-progress, should study. Such works as those of Mason on Self-Knowledge, Burgh on the Dignity of Human Nature, Watts on the Mind, Opie on Detraction and Scandal, Wayland on Moral Science, Skinner on the Religion of the Bible, &c. &c., should not only be perused, but carefully studied. It is to little purpose, that is, comparatively, that our physical nature is attentively and assiduously studied and cultivated, if it lead not to the more intimate and more earnest study of the immortal spirit.

In this better department—the spiritual—permit me, *once* more, to direct your attention to the Bible. It should be studied chiefly without note or comment. Your own good sense, brought to bear upon its simple, unstudied, unscholastic pages, accompanied by that light from on high which is ever vouchsafed to the simple, humble inquirer and learner, will be of more value to you than all the notes, and commentaries, and dictionaries in the world, without it. It is a book which is most admirably adapted to the progress of all grades of mind—those which are but little developed, no less than those which are more highly cultivated. Other books speak to the intellect—to the head; this speaks to the heart. Other books often plead for human nature; this presents it just as it is—its perversity and deformity on the one side; its susceptibilities to improvement, its capability of excellency, on the other. Though it reveals to us our humble origin—the brotherhood of worms—on the one side, it unveils to us our relation to angels and archangels, on the other. Nay, more; it not only shows us our relation to the celestial hosts, and to Him who presides in their midst, but it points out to the penitent and the humble, the road which, through divine grace, will conduct them thither.

I have spoken of the study of the Bible without note or comment. Notes and comments, indeed, after you have made diligent use of all your own faculties and powers, and sought thereon the blessing of God's Spirit, have their use. I am exceedingly fond of them: and I would not wholly deny to you what I am so fond of myself. The danger is, of leaning upon them too much. Scott, and Clarke, and Henry, and Jenks, and Calmet, and Barnes, and Bush, may help to show me the true way of finding out and interpreting the Scripture for myself; but if I go farther, and either indolently or superstitiously suffer them to interpret it for me, it were almost better that I had not sought their aid. But the Bible, with or without notes, is—I repeat it—the great volume of self-knowledge which I urge you to study, and which, in comparison with all the books written by man, and even the great volume of nature herself, is alone able to make you wise to salvation.

It seems to me to have been too seldom observed, and still more seldom insisted on, how apt the love and study of the Bible are to awaken the dormant intellectual faculties, and to enkindle, even in the aged, a desire for general improvement. On this point, Mr. Foster, in his essay on Popular Ignorance, has some very striking remarks. In alluding to that great moral change which it is one object of the Bible to produce, and to the consequences which often immediately follow, he thus remarks:

"It is exceedingly striking to observe how the contracted, rigid soul seems to soften, and grow warm, and expand, and quiver with life. With the new energy infused, it painfully struggles to work itself into freedom from the wretched contortion in which it has been so long fixed, as by the impressed spell of infernal magic."

This change in the moral and religious man, has been often observed; and Mr. Foster, therefore, tells us nothing very new, however striking it may be. But now for the secondary effect which is produced on the intellect, and, indeed, on the whole character:

"It (the soul) has been seen filled with a painful and indignant emotion at its own ignorance; actuated with a restless desire to be informed; acquiring an unwonted applicableness of its faculties to thought; attaining a perception combined of intelligence and moral sensibility, to which numerous things are becoming discernible and affecting, that were as non-existent before. We have known instances in which the change—the intellectual change—has been so conspicuous, within a brief space of time, that even an infidel observer must have forfeited all claim to a man of sense, if he would not make the acknowledgment—This that you call divine grace, whatever it may really be, is the strangest awakener of faculties, after all."

I have made this quotation, chiefly to confirm the sentiment I have advanced, that the love of the Bible and the religion of the Bible, actuates the soul with "a restless desire to be informed," and stimulates its faculties to thought, and fills it with pain and indignation at its own ignorance. This is the state of mind and heart which I would gladly encourage in the reader. It is the truest and best foundation of all progress, not only in self-knowledge, but in every other sort of knowledge which is valuable. Give me but this trait of character in a young woman, and I will not despair of her, however low may be her present condition, or how degraded soever may have been her former life. Give me but a hearty desire, a hungering and thirsting for improvement—physical, moral, intellectual, social and religious—and I will dare to believe that the most debased and depressed soul *may* be restored, at least in some good measure, to that likeness to Jehovah in which it was originally created.

One thing more, however, should be remembered. Not a few who really have within them the desire of improvement, and who mean to make the Bible and its doctrines their standard, fail of accomplishing much after all. The reason is, they measure themselves, continually, by their neighbors. If they are no more ignorant or no more vicious than their neighbors—Misses S. and L., perhaps—or on the other hand, if they are as wise and as virtuous as Miss R.—they seem to rest satisfied. Or at any rate, if, they make as much progress in the great path of self-knowledge, or do as much good in the world as the latter, they are anxious for no more, and settle down in inaction.

Now every such individual ought to know that the habit of measuring herself by others, in this way, will hang like a millstone about her neck; and if it do not drown her in the depths of ignorance and imbecility, will at least make her forever a child, in comparison with what she should be. It will keep her grovelling on the earth's surface, when she ought to be exploring the highest heavens. It will keep her a near neighbor to the sisterhood of worms on which she treads, when she ought to be soaring towards those lofty heights which Gabriel once traversed—nay, which he even now traverses—fast by the throne of the Eternal.

Let her not stop, then, to demean, and embarrass, and fetter herself by comparisons of herself with any thing finite. She has no right to do this. The perfection which the word of God requires, is the standard or measure by which she should compare herself. She may, indeed, sometimes compare herself with herself—her present self with her past self—provided it be done with due humility; but let her beware of measuring herself by others. Such a course is as perilous as it is ignoble and unprofitable.

CHAPTER VI.

CONSCIENTIOUSNESS.

Is there any conscientiousness in the world? How far conscientiousness should extend. Tendency and power of habit Evils of doing incessantly what we know to be wrong. Why we do this. Errors of early education. False standard of right and wrong. Bad method of family discipline. Palsy of the moral sensibilities. Particular direction in regard to the education of the conscience. Results which may be expected.

There is such a want of conscientiousness among mankind, even among those who are professedly good people, that one might almost be pardoned for concluding that there is either no conscience in the world, or that the heavenly monitor is at least no where fully obeyed. For is there not too much foundation for such a conclusion?

While truth compels us to admit that Christianity has already done much to awaken the consciences of men, we shall gain nothing by shutting our eyes to the vast influence it has yet to exert, before mankind will become what they ought to be.

Most people are conscientious in *some* things. They may have been so trained, for instance, that they are quite tender in regard to the feelings of others, and even those of animals. There are many who, with Cowper, "would not enter on their list of friends the man who needlessly sets foot upon a worm," who are yet very far from possessing much real conscientiousness. Their feeling is better entitled to the name of *sympathy*.

I grant that many of these persons possess something more than mere tenderness or sympathy. Not a few of them are truly conscientious in what may be called the larger concerns of life—especially in external religion. They not only feel the force of conscience, but they obey her voice in some things. They would not fail to attend to all the outward rites of religion in the most faithful manner, on any account whatever; and if a failure should occur, would find their consciences reproaching them in the severest manner, for their departures from a known standard of duty.

These persons regard, with a considerable degree of conscientiousness, the law of the land and the law of public opinion, or at least the law of fashion. In respect to any thing which would subject them to the severity of public remark, or which would even be regarded by the coarse, public eye, as glaringly inconsistent with their religious character, they are never wanting in sensibility. Their consciences reproach them, when they have done or said any thing which may cause them to be ill spoken of.

Thus far, it cannot be denied that there is a great deal of conscientiousness in the world. But beyond limits something like these, it is much more rare than many suppose. To say that it does not exist beyond such narrow limits, would be unjust; but it must be admitted that, taking the world at large, its existence is so rare, as hardly to entitle it to the name of a living, moving, breathing principle of action.

I do not suppose that young women are less conscientious than young men; nor that the young of either sex are less conscientious than their seniors. It would be a novel if not unheard of thing, to find the youth without conscience, merging, in due time, into the conscientious octogenarian. The contrary is the more common course.

And yet how few are the young women who make it a matter of conscience to perform every thing they do—the smaller no less than the larger matters of life—in such a way as to meet the approbation of an internal monitor. Do they not generally bow to the tribunal of a fashionable world? Do they generally care sufficiently, in the every day actions, words, thoughts and feelings of their lives, what God's vicegerent in the soul says about their conduct?—or if they *do* care, is it because it is right or wrong in the sight of God—or of *man*?

A due regard to the authority of conscience would lead people, as it seems to me, to yield obedience to her dictates on every occasion. They who disregard her voice in one thing, are likely to do so in others. Who does not know the power of habit? Who will deny that the individual who habitually disregards the voice speaking within, on a particular subject will be likely, ere long, to extend the same habit of disregard to something else; and thus on to the end of the chapter, if any end there be to it?

No one, it is believed, will doubt that I have rightly described the tendency of habit in large matters. He who would allow himself to steal from day to day, unmindful of the voice within which bids him beware, would not only, ere long, if unmolested, come to a point at which conscience would cease to reproach him, but would be likely to venture upon other kinds of wrong. I have seen those who would habitually steal small things, and yet would not tell a lie for the world. But I have known the habit of stealing continue till lying also gradually came to be a habit, and was scarcely thought of as offensive in the sight of God, or as positively wrong in the nature of things, any more than picking up a basket of pebbles. From lying, the natural transition is to profanity—and so on, till conscience, chased up and down like the last lonely deer of a forest, at length exhausted, faints and dies.

Few, I say, will deny the tendency and power of habit, in regard to the larger matters of life. But is it sufficiently known that every act which can possibly be regarded as fraudulent in the smallest degree, has the same tendency?

There are a thousand things that people do, which cannot be set down as absolutely criminal, in the view of human law, or human courts, and which are not forbidden in any particular chapter or verse of the divine law, which, notwithstanding, are forbidden by the spirit of both.

Human law, no less than divine law, requires us to love our neighbor as ourselves. Is the law obeyed when we make the smallest approach to taking that advantage of a neighbor, which we would not like to have taken of us in similar circumstances?

Those who admit and seem to understand the power of habit in larger matters, are yet prone to forget the tendency of an habitual disregard of right and wrong in small matters. They are by no means ignorant, that large rivers are made up of springs, and rills, and brooks; but they do not seem to consider that the larger stream of conscientiousness must also be fed by its thousand tributaries, or it will never flow; or once flowing, will be likely soon to cease. In other words, to be conscientious—truly so—in the larger and more important concerns of life, we must be habitually, and I had almost said religiously so, in smaller matters—in our most common and every day concerns.

Would that nothing worse were true, than that people of all ranks and professions, and of all ages and conditions, habitually, and with less and less compunction or regret, do that which they know they ought not to do, and leave undone that which they very well know ought to be done. For they even seem to justify themselves in it.

> "I know the right, and I approve it too;
> I know the wrong, and yet the wrong pursue"—

is the language of many an individual—even of some from whom we could hope better things; and not a few charge it upon the frailty of fallen nature—as that nature now is—independent of, and in spite of their own efforts! Strange infatuation!

One way of solving this great riddle in human life and conduct—this incessant doing by mankind of that which they know they ought not to do, and neglecting to do that which they know ought to be done—may be found in the fact that so few are trained to regard, in every thing, the sacred rights of conscience. They are referred to other and more questionable standards of authority.

If you do so and so, you will never be a lady, says a mother who wishes to dissuade her young daughter from doing something to which she is inclined. If you behave so, every body will laugh at you, says another. If you do not obey me, I shall punish you, says a third. If you don't do that, I shall tell mother, says a young brother or sister. If you do not do it, father will give you no sugar toys, when he comes home, the child is again told. If you don't mind me, the bears will come and eat you up, says the petulant nurse or maid-servant. Thus, in one way or another, and at one time or another, every motive—love, fear, selfishness, pleasure, &c.—is appealed to in the education of the young, except that which should be *chiefly* appealed to—viz., self-approbation, or the approbation of conscience.

This is not all. There is with many of these people no settled rule as to which sort of actions are to be the subjects of praise or of blame. A thing which must not be done to-day, on penalty of the loss of the forthcoming sugar toys, is connived at, perhaps with a kiss, to-morrow. All in the child's mind is confusion; she knows not what to do, were she as docile and as obedient as an angel of light. There is a long series of actions, words, thoughts and feelings, connected with right and wrong, of which nothing is ever said, except to forbid them, by stern and absolute authority. That one is good, and another bad, except according to the whim or fancy of the parent or teacher, the child never suspects.

Of this last class are almost all the actions of every-day life. The child alluded to is scolded, at times, for default in matters which pertain to rising, dressing, saying prayers, eating, drinking, playing, speaking, running, teazing, or soiling its clothes or books, and a thousand things too familiar to every one to render it necessary to repeat.

Perhaps she eats too much, or eats greedily; or she inclines to be slovenly, or indolent, or fretful. Now all these things are in general merely forbidden or *rated*, or at most, shown to be contrary to the will of the parents. They are seldom or never shown to be right or wrong, in their own nature; nor is the child assured, upon the authority of the parent, that there is a natural right or wrong to them. Thus, what is not implanted, does not, of course, grow. All the little actions and concerns of life, or almost all—and these, by their number and frequent recurrence, make up almost the whole of a child's existence—are, as it were, left wholly without the domain of conscience; and the young woman grows up to maturity without a distinct conviction that conscience has any thing to do with them.

And "what is bred in the bone," according to a vulgar maxim, "stays long in the flesh." As is the child, so is the adult. It is one of the most difficult things in the world to make a person conscientious in all things, who has not been trained to be so. Hence the great difficulty in the way of making every-day Christians. Our religion is thought by some to have nothing to do with these ever-recurring small matters. And when we are told that we should do every thing to the honor and glory of God, although we may assent to the proposition, it is hard to put it in practice. There is a sort of moral palsy prevailing in the community—and that, too, very extensively.

No fatal error of early education could have seized more firmly, or palsied more effectually the moral sensibilities of the whole community, than this. And therefore it is certain that this is at least one principal reason why there is so little conscience in the world, and why it is so often a starveling wherever it is found to exist.

I have heard an eminent teacher contend with much earnestness, that there is a great multitude of the smaller actions of human life which are destitute of character—wholly so. They are, he says, neither right nor wrong. But if so, then is there no responsibility attached to them; and, consequently, no conscientiousness required in connection with their due performance. But what, in that case, is to become of the injunction of a distinguished apostle, when he says, WHATEVER you do, do all to the glory of God? If every thing we do should be done to the glory of God, and not thus to do it, is to disobey a righteous precept, then there is a right and wrong in every thing. Now which shall we believe—the human teacher or the divine?

This origin of a common error, I have deemed it necessary for every young woman to understand, that she may know how to apply the correction, and where to begin. She should love and respect her parents, even if they belong to the class which has been described. She should consider the present imperfect state of human nature, and be thankful for the thousand benefits she has received at their hands, and the various means of improvement within her reach.

If she has drank deeply of the desire for improvement, and if she wishes to know and to reform herself as fast as possible, let her begin by cultivating, to the highest possible degree, a sense of right and wrong, and an implicit and unwavering obedience to the right.

Before closing this chapter, however, I wish to present a few illustrations of my meaning, when I say that every thing should be done in a conscientious manner. Perhaps, indeed, I am already sufficiently understood; but lest I should not be by all, I subjoin the following.

Suppose a young woman is in the habit of lying in bed late in the morning. In view of her varied responsibilities and of the vast importance of rising early, and with a strong desire for continual improvement, she sets herself to change the habit.

Now to aid her in her task—for it is no light one—let her endeavor to consider the whole matter. God gives us sleep, she will perhaps say to herself, for the restoration of our bodies and minds; and all the time really necessary for this is well employed. But I have found that I feel better, and actually enjoy myself better, for the whole day following, when, by accident or by any other means, I have slept an hour less than I am accustomed to do. I usually sleep nine hours or more, whereas I am quite sure eight are sufficient for every reasonable purpose.

Moreover, if I sleep an hour too much, that hour is wasted. Have I a right to waste it? It is God's gift; is it not slighting his gift, to spend it in sleep? Is it not a sin? And to do so day after day and year after year, is it not to make myself exceedingly guilty in his sight? One hour, daily saved for the purpose of reading or study, after a person has really slept enough, is equal, in sixteen years, to the addition of a full year to one's life. Can it be that I waste, in sleep, in fifteen or sixteen years, a whole year of time?

I must do so no longer. It injures my complexion; it injures my health; it is an indolent practice: but above all, it is a sin against God.

I am resolved to redeem my time. And to aid me in this work, I am determined, if I fail in any instance, to remember this decision, and the grounds on which it was made.

She carries out her decision. She finds herself waking too late, occasionally, it is true. However, she not only hurries out of bed the instant she wakes, but recalls her former view of the sinfulness of her conduct. She is no sooner dressed, than she asks pardon for her transgression, and prays that she may transgress no more. This course she continues; and thus her convictions of the sinfulness of her former indolent habit and waste of time are deepened. At length, by her persevering efforts and the assistance of God, she gains the victory, and a new and better habit is completely established.

Just so should it be with any other bad habit. Every young woman should consider it as a sin against God, and should begin the work of reformation as a duty, not only to herself and to others, but also and more especially to God. If it be nothing but the error of eating too much—which, by the way, is not so small an error as many seem to suppose—let her try to regard it in its true light, as a transgression against the laws of God. Let it be so regarded, not merely once or twice, but habitually. In this way it will soon become— as in the case of early rising—a matter of conscience.

The close of the day, however, is a specially important season for cultivating the habit of conscientiousness. Sleep is the image of death, as some have said; and if so, we may consider ourselves at bed-time, as standing on the borders of the grave, where all things should look serious.

The "cool of the day" is peculiarly adapted to reflection. Let every one, at this time, recall the circumstances of the day, and consider wherein things have been wrong. It was a sacred rule among the Pythagoreans, every evening, to run thrice over, in their minds, the events of the day; and shall Christians do less than heathen?

The Pythagoreans did more than cultivate a habit of recalling their errors; they asked themselves what good they had done. So should we. We should remember that it is not only sinful to do wrong, but that it is also sinful to *omit to do right.* The young woman who fears she has said something in regard to a fellow being in a certain place, or in certain company, which she ought not to have said, as it may do that person injury, should remember, that not to have said something, when a favorable opportunity offered, which might have done a companion or neighbor good, was also equally wrong. And above all, she should remember, that both the *commission* and the *omission* were sins against that God who gave her a tongue to do good with, and not to do harm; and not only to do good with, but to do the greatest possible amount of good.

In short, it should be the constant practice of every one who has the love of eternal improvement strongly implanted in her bosom, to consider every action performed, during the day, as sinful, when it has not been done in the best possible manner, whether it may have been one thing or another. As I have stated repeatedly elsewhere, there is nothing worth doing at all, which should not be done to the honor and glory of God; and she who would attain to the highest measure of perfection, should regard nothing as done in this manner, which is not done exactly as God her Saviour would have it done.

It is desirable not only to avoid benumbing or searing over the conscience, but that we should cultivate it to the highest possible tenderness. True, these tender consciences are rather *troublesome*; but is it not better that they should torture us a little now, than a great deal hereafter?

I have said that some good people—that is, those who are comparatively good—fall short in this matter. A young woman is a teacher, perhaps, in a Sabbath school. She knows, full well, the importance of attending promptly at the appointed hour; and she makes it a point thus to attend. At last she fails, on a single occasion—not from necessity, but from negligence, or at least from want of due care—and her conscience at once reproaches her for her conduct. But, ere long, the offence is repeated. The reproaches of her conscience, though still felt, have become less keen. The offence is repeated, again and again, till conscience is almost seared over—and the omission of what had at first given great pain, almost ceases to be troublesome. And thus the conscience, having been blunted in one respect, is more liable to be so in others. Alas for the individual, who is thus, from day to day, growing worse, and yet from day to day becoming less sensible of it!

But there is a worse case than I have yet mentioned. A young woman has risen rather late on Sunday morning; and having risen late, other things are liable to be late. The hour for church is at length near; the bell is even ringing. Something in the way of dress, not very necessary except to comply with fashion, and yet on the whole desirable, remains to be done during the remaining five minutes; but what is more important still, the habit of secret prayer for five minutes before going to church, is uncomplied with. One of these, the closet or the dress, must be neglected for want of time. Does any one doubt which it will be? Does any one doubt that the dress will receive the desired attention, and that the closet will be neglected?

But does any one suppose that conscientiousness can live and flourish where it is not only not cultivated, but habitually violated, in regard to the most sacred matters? Secret prayer is one of the most sacred duties; and they who habitually neglect or violate it, for the salve of doing that which is of secondary importance—knowing it to be so—are not only taking the sure course to eradicate all conscientiousness from their bosoms, but are most manifestly preferring the world to God, and the love and service of the world, to the love and service of its glorious Creator and Redeemer.

Let me say, in concluding this chapter, that if the conscience is cultivated from day to day, it will, in time, acquire a degree of tenderness and accuracy to which most of the world are entire strangers. There is, however, one thing more, Conscience will not only become more tender and faithful, but her *domain* will be much enlarged by the study of the Bible; and in many cases is which this heavenly monitor was once silent, she will now utter her warning voice. Conscience is not unalterable, as some suppose she is susceptible of elevation as long as we live; and happy is the individual who elevates her to her rightful throne. Happy is the individual who sees things most nearly as God sees them, and whose conscience condemns her in every thing which is contrary to the divine will.

CHAPTER VII.

SELF-GOVERNMENT.

What self-government includes. Cheerfulness a duty. Discretion. Modesty. Diffidence. Courage. Vigilance. Thoughts and feelings. The affections. The temper. The appetites and passions.

This is so broad a subject that I shall present my thoughts concerning it under several different heads. It includes, in my estimation, the government of the THOUGHTS, the IMAGINATION, the TEMPER, the AFFECTIONS, and the APPETITES. The young woman who truly governs herself, will be at once *cheerful, discreet, modest, diffident, vigilant, courageous, active, temperate* and *happy.*

Cheerfulness.—Is cheerfulness within our power? some may be inclined to ask. I certainly regard it so. That there are moments of our lives—nay, even considerable seasons—when cheerfulness is not required, may, indeed, be true. Our friends sicken and die, and we mourn for them. This is a law of our nature. Even our Saviour was, at times, a man of sorrows and acquainted with grief; though of all individuals in the universe cheerfulness was his right. But he bore more than his own sorrows; and in so far as his example is, in this respect, binding upon us, it is only when we bear the sorrows of others. Those should, indeed, often be borne; and in proportion as they are borne—in proportion as we are wounded for the transgressions, and bruised for the iniquities of others—it may not be possible for us to be continually cheerful.

As for our own sorrows—the sufferings, the pangs, the bereavements of our own existence—we should never cease to regard them, in some measure, at least, as the chastisements of an Almighty Father. Smitten friends, according to the sentiment of a distinguished poet, are messengers of mercy to us—are sent on errands full of love.

"For us they sicken, and for us they die."

We should be at least resigned, even under such chastisements, when we remember they are inflicted by a Father's hand.

But setting aside occasions of this kind, is there not a demand on our whole nature, for general cheerfulness? It is not only the "sunshine of the soul," but that of the body. The truly cheerful are not only happier in their minds and spirits, but also in their very bodies. The brain and nervous system play their part in the great drama of physical life better; the heart, and stomach, and lungs, work better. Indeed, all is better throughout.

Is not that a duty which is productive of so much happiness? But can that be a duty which it is not in our power to perform? It were surely an impeachment of the wisdom and goodness of God, did he require us, in his providence or in his word—by his natural or his revealed law—to do that of which we are incapable.

I consider cheerfulness, then, as a matter of duty; and, of course, as in a great measure in our power. It makes us happier ourselves; it enables us to reflect more happiness on others. I consider it especially as a duty of the young, who have it in their power to communicate happiness thereby in such large measure. Let them—let young women especially—strive to cultivate it. It is in its nature a perennial plant; and if it is not such at the present time, it is because it has degenerated in a degenerate world. Let it be restored to its pristine beauty; and let the world thereby—in connection with other means tending to the same end— be restored to what it was before the loss of Eden.

Discretion.—This is a virtue with which, it is supposed by some, the young have little if any thing to do. I cannot assent to such an opinion. I believe that the young are to be trained in the way they should go; and as discretion is prominently a virtue of middle and later life, I deem it desirable that we should see at least the germs of it in the young.

Above all, do I like to see the young woman discreet. Discretion not only heightens the pleasures of her existence, but adds greatly to her reputation in the just estimation of the wise. Coupled with modesty, of which I am to speak presently, it more than doubles her charms.

Let discretion then be studied. Let it be studied, too, for its immediate as well as remote benefits. It will, indeed, bear fruit more abundantly in later life; but it will not be without its value in youth. It is a plant which it were worth while to cultivate, if human existence were more frail, and life more uncertain of continuance than it now is.

MODESTY.—Of all the qualities appropriate to young women, I know of none which is more universally esteemed than modesty. And what has been, by common consent, so highly esteemed, I cannot find it in my heart to under-value. Indeed, I do not think it has ever been over-valued, or that it can be.

I have been somewhat amused—not to say instructed—by the following remarks on this trait of female character, from the pen of one who is, not only a philosopher, but a physiologist. [Footnote: Alexander Walker, the author of several British works connected with the subject of physical education and physical improvement.] They are not the more interesting, perhaps, because they are somewhat new; but neither are they less so. As I have nothing else to say on this topic, which has not been said a thousand times, I transcribe the more freely, the thoughts of the author to whom I refer.

"Modesty establishes an equilibrium between the superiority of man and the delicacy of woman; it enables woman to insure thereby for herself, a supporter—a defender. And while man thus barters his protection for love, woman is a match for his power; and the weaker, to a great extent, governs the stronger."

"It is probable that modesty derives its cause in woman, from a certain mistrust in her own merit, and from the fear of finding herself below that very affection which she is capable of exciting, and of which she is the object. ... Modesty compels her love to assume that form by which nature has taught her so universally to express it—that of gratitude, friendship, &c. ... Modesty is a means of attraction with which nature inspires all females."

Under this head I will just add, that since by modesty the weaker govern the stronger, it is of immense importance that woman should know the true secret of maintaining her power and also by what means she is likely to jeopardize that power. And without undertaking to determine what shall be the precise rules of female action, and the precise limits of the sphere within which the Author of her nature designed she should move, is it not worth the serious inquiry, whether she does not, as a general fact, lose influence the moment she departs widely from the province which God in nature seems to have allotted her; when, like a Woolstoncroft, or a Wright, or others still of less painful notoriety, she mounts the rostrum, and becomes the centre of gaping, perhaps admiring thousands of the other sex, as well as of her own. So did not the excellent women of Galilee, eighteen hundred years ago; although they were engaged, heart and hand, in a cause than which none could be more glorious, or afford a greater triumph, especially to their own sex. They probably knew too well their power, to endanger it thus in the general scale; or if not, they probably yielded to the impulses of a spirit which could direct them in a path more congenial to their own nature, as well as on the whole more conducive to their own emancipation, elevation and perfection.

DIFFIDENCE.—This trait, though nearly related to modesty, is far from being the same thing, its character having been more frequently brought in question than that of modesty. And yet it seems to me equally valuable. It gilds what modesty graces; and polishes what modesty improves.

Let not the reader confound modesty and bashfulness; for they are by no means the same thing. Modesty is as much opposed to impudence as any thing can be; and yet it is certain that impudence is often conjoined with bashfulness. Not so often, to be sure, in the female sex, as in our own; and yet such a phenomenon is occasionally witnessed, even in woman.

Bashfulness is usually the result of too low an estimate of ourselves; whereas, true diffidence only leads us to value ourselves according to our real worth. Diffidence makes us humble, but bashfulness sometimes makes us mean; at least, there is danger of it. It is, at all events, of doubtful utility; and though I would not denounce or condemn it, I would urge the young to endeavor to rise far above it.

But I repeat it—I would endeavor to cultivate and encourage every thing which belongs to true diffidence. It will assist modesty in performing her angelic office; and the influence of both, united, may save from many a pang in this world, and perhaps prove a means, under God, of preventing the sentence of condemnation in the world to come.

COURAGE.—By courage I do not mean that trait for which man is constitutionally as much distinguished, as woman is for the want of it I mean not a courage to meet and surmount physical difficulties, and encounter outward and physical dangers. I mean, on the contrary, that moral courage which is neither confined to sex nor condition.

Not that physical courage is to be despised, even by females. On the contrary, I think it is a trait of character which is quite too much neglected in female education. It is not only lamentable, but pitiable, to see a female of twenty, thirty, or fifty years of age, shrinking at the sight of a spider, or a toad, even when there is not the smallest prospect of its coming within three yards of her. Nor is it as it should be, when a young woman, already eighteen or twenty years of age, has such a dread of pigs and cows, as to scream aloud at the sight of one in a field, so well enclosed that it is not possible her safety could be endangered were the animal ever so malicious. Such unreasonable and foolish fears ought by no means to be encouraged; on the contrary, she who finds herself a slave to them, ought to suppress them as fast as possible.

This is, indeed, an important but much neglected part of female education; and she who is a sufferer therefrom, will do well to derive a hint from these pages. The unreasonable fears of which I speak, are by no means confined to the sight of toads, or spiders, or pigs, or cows. We find them more or less frequently, and in some form or other, in nearly every family. Some are unreasonably afraid of dogs and horses; others, of cats or snakes; others, again, of the dark, or of being alone by night or by day.

Let me not be understood as saying that no tears are to be indulged, in regard to any of these things; it is only an unreasonable and foolish degree of fear, that should be guarded against. A cow or a horse feeding quietly in a pasture, and separated from you by a stout fence, which no animal in any ordinary circumstances is wont to leap, is not a proper object of fear with a rational person over twelve years of age. If a cow or horse is running at large in the highway, and appears fearless of man, or furious, or if mad dogs are about, enough of fear may reasonably be indulged to keep you from the streets, and confine you to your home, unless you have suitable protection.

But as I have already said, it is *moral* courage that I would inspire in the young woman. She has patience, and perseverance, and fortitude—why then may she not add to these, moral courage? What man has done, man may do—has been a thousand times said; and the remark is not less applicable to woman than to man. What woman has done, woman may do. But woman, in numerous instances, has possessed moral courage. She has been known, more than once, to "face a frowning world," or to oppose some of its tyrant fashions. I could mention more than one who has thus evinced true moral courage, and set her sex a glorious example, which not a few of my readers might do well to follow.

Let woman dare to do right—whether fashionable or unfashionable. Let her dare to do so in the smaller no less than in the larger matters of life. Let her dare to obey God, and the laws of God, both natural and revealed—both within and around her—rather than the laws of any man or set of men. Let her do this, and she will evince true moral courage; a courage as far surpassing the highest efforts of physical courage of prowess, as right surpasses might; virtue, vice; or purity, impurity.

VIGILANCE.—The young woman who truly understands and practises the art of self-government, will not only train herself to be at once cheerful, discreet, modest, diffident and courageous; she will also be vigilant. The largest ship may be sunk by a very small leak; and in like manner, may the brightest and noblest character lose its lustre, unless the possessor is ever on the watch. Let not the most perfect individual on earth say, in the plenitude of his own power, and in the height of his own assurance—"My mountain stands strong. I shall never be moved." Such assurances of self-government and self-possession may be proper—of course are so—in Him who is in his own nature perfect and immutable—infinitely and eternally so; but not in a frail, mutable, created man or woman—above all, in the young and inexperienced.

Pardon me, then, youthful reader, when I repeat the Scripture cautions—"Be vigilant;" and "Let him who thinketh he standeth, take heed lest he fall." It is easier to maintain the measure of self-government we have already attained, and even to add to it, than to recover what we have once lost.

THOUGHTS AND FEELINGS.—On this account, set a guard over the very thoughts of your hearts. All sin begins in the desires of the heart and the affections of the soul. There, in the deep recesses of the man, it germinates. Let every imagination, then, which exalts itself unduly, be brought low; and let the stream of thought and feeling be pure, and perfect, and holy. Acquire the exceedingly important habit of confining your thoughts and desires to those subjects which your judgment tells you are lawful and proper—and which are not only lawful and proper in general, but which are so at particular times and places. The wise man says there is a time and season for every thing; and more than intimates, that it is wisdom to confine every thing—thoughts and feelings, no less than words and actions—to their own place and time, respectively.

But to learn to think with *order,* is one exceedingly important item in the art of *governing* our thoughts. Half the thought in the world is of a mere random character. Men are but half men who have not yet attained to the government of their thoughts and feelings.

THE AFFECTIONS.—Even these, as I have already said, can be controlled. Were it not so, what meaning would there be in the gospel commands—so incessantly repeated by the divine Author of the gospel—to love our *enemies?* On this subject—the regulation, and if I may so say, the application of the affections—I intend to dwell at greater length hereafter.

THE TEMPER.—Nothing is more unpleasant—slovenliness, perhaps, excepted—than a bad temper. I beseech every one who is so unhappy as to possess such a temper, to pay particular attention to what I am about to say, on this interesting and important topic.

Some young women seem entirely to overlook the consequences of an ill temper. These are numerous—too numerous to be mentioned in a single chapter. I shall only say here, that such a temper is no less destructive—in a slow way—to the health of the body, than it is to the mental faculties and the affections.

Some suppose their ill temper to be constitutional, and this serves them as an apology for neglecting to govern it. They seem to regard it as so wrought into their very structure, that it will hardly be possible ever to eradicate it. They are condemned by inheritance, as they appear to suppose, to a perpetual war within—in which the most they can hope for is an occasional victory.

Now let me tell every young woman who has imbibed this erroneous and dangerous notion, that God has never suffered the command of her temper to be placed beyond her reach. She may acquire the most perfect self-command, even in this respect, if she will. Not in a moment, nor in a day, it is true. The work may be the labor of months, or of years. Still, the battle can be won: a permanent and final victory can be achieved.

The very general idea, that single persons somewhat advanced in life, especially females, become habitually impatient or ill tempered, has too much truth for its foundation, though it is by no means universally true. Nor is it ever necessary that it should be so, as I have endeavored to show elsewhere.

I wish every young person could be induced to study deeply the causes which operate on mankind to originate or perpetuate a bad temper. They are numerous—exceedingly so. It is not necessary to charge much upon our ancestors. The causes may much oftener be found within our own minds and bodies, would we but look for them there. We harbor or perhaps indulge a thousand unpleasant feelings from day to day, not seeming to know, or at least to realize, that as small streams form larger ones, so these first risings of anger lead to its more out-breaking forms.

Not a few of the instances of irritability, fretfulness, impatience and melancholy, have their origin in physical causes—in errors in regard to exercise, sleep, air, temperature, dress, eating, drinking, &c.; and some have their origin in mistakes about the theory or the practice of religion. Some originate, too, in disappointed love. In short, their sources are well nigh endless.

THE APPETITES AND PASSIONS.—It is in vain, or almost in vain, to hope for any radical improvement in our physical, intellectual or moral condition, except in proportion as the body and the bodily appetites are kept in proper subjection to right reason and religion.

Here I must again urge upon every young woman the duty of studying the laws of health, and especially those of temperance. The knowledge thus to be obtained, would be of exceeding great value to her in the government of her passions and appetites.

Prof. Mussey, recently of Dartmouth College, in New Hampshire, relates, that a teacher in Boston, whose general course of discipline was quite mild, was sometimes so much affected in his temper by high-seasoned or over-stimulating dinners, as to be petulant and passionate, even to blows, immediately afterward.

Now, whether this was often the case with the individual in question, I cannot say. This, however, I may affirm with the utmost safety and confidence—that many an individual who finds her passions or her appetites more than usually troublesome or rebellious, would do well to look for the cause in the bad air which she breathes, the bad food or drinks she uses, or in something else in herself or in her habits which might have been prevented.

Sometimes tea or coffee, notwithstanding their first effects to enliven, produce the results I have mentioned, as their secondary effects. Sometimes a hearty dinner of flesh meat, or a more moderate one, with bad accompaniments, or with improper seasonings, is the cause of trouble. Sometimes the cause is something either quite indigestible, or difficult of digestion, whether it be animal or vegetable. And, lastly, but yet most frequently of all, it may be excess of quantity, or the bad cooking of substances naturally wholesome and digestible.

I press this part of my subject upon the consideration of young women, because it concerns not them alone, but a host of others. No one liveth to himself, says an apostle; and the remark is quite as important in its application to the young woman, as to any other individual.

One reason why I urge it is, because we are almost universally referred to moral means and moral considerations alone, in order to keep in subjection the body—its passions and appetites—and seldom, if ever, to a proper attention to our food or our drink, our air, our exercise, or our sleep. Nay, the hopes of the young, in regard to keeping the body in subjection, are sometimes completely paralyzed by the grave assertion, that the strength of our passions and appetites is constitutional—as much our inheritance, as the color of our eyes, or the contour of our physiognomies, and almost equally unalterable.

Now I would encourage no young woman to expect too much of "temperance in all things," without the co-operation of the moral powers, and especially of the will. But I would encourage her to strict temperance for her own sake, and that of others. I would say to her once more, that in proportion to her obedience to the laws of health, in regard to air, exercise, sleep, temperature, study, food, drink, clothing, &c., &c., will be her ability to govern herself according to right, and reason, and the commands of the Creator. The simpler her diet, for example, and the more free it is from extraneous things—as fat, condiments, &c.—the easier will it be to keep herself in proper subjection to herself—the body to the immortal spirit.

One of the most powerful and ever active causes of that slavery of the soul to the body, which every person of sense must perceive and deplore, is our unnatural and artificial cookery. Had it been the aim of all the cookery in the world, to make it as bad as possible for the health of body and soul, I know not that things could have been worse than they are now. Very few things, indeed, are made more palatable, more digestible, or more nutritious by it—the legitimate and only ends of all the efforts of our fashionable cookery. On the contrary, they are made, almost universally, a great deal worse for us.

Let the young woman who would serve God in her day and generation, by doing good in the reformation, elevation, and eternal progress of herself and those around her, not only study deeply the laws of health and life, but let her tax her powers of reasoning and invention, to see if it is not possible to remove the cause of so much mischief from our parlors, our sleeping-rooms, our kitchens, and our tables. Much must be done, in this respect, before the world can become what it ought to be; and woman must lead the way—woman of some future generation, if not of the present.

CHAPTER VIII.

Presence of mind. Examples. Napoleon. Female example. Mrs. Merrill. Use of the anecdote. Self-command to be cultivated. In what manner Consult the experience of others. Consult your own reason and good sense. Daily practice in the art of self-command.

I was, at first, disposed to call this chapter Presence of Mind; but for various reasons, I have chosen to call it by another name—that of Self-Command.

To acquire the art of properly commanding ourselves, in all circumstances—especially in the most trying emergencies, and at a moment of danger, when not a minute, perhaps not a second, should be lost—is as difficult as it is important to every person; and to none perhaps more so, than to young women. Not that their trials of this sort will be more frequent than those of other people; but because the usual course of their education is such as to prepare them but poorly to meet those which fall to their lot.

It is said that Napoleon was greatly distinguished for the trait of character of which I am now speaking. But there are also numerous. examples of self-command in females on record. I will relate one.

Some thirty or forty years ago, when the Indians had not yet done making depredations on the inhabitants of our then frontier states, Kentucky and Ohio, a band of these savage men came to the door of a house in Nelson county, Ky., and having shot down the father of the little family within, who had incautiously opened the door, they attempted to rush in and put to death the defenceless and unoffending mother and her children. But Mrs. Merrill—for that was the name of the heroic woman—had much of that self-command, or presence of mind, which was now so needful. She drew her wounded husband into the house, closed the door and barred it as quickly as possible, so that the Indians could not enter at once, and then proceeded to the defence of "her castle," and all those in it whom she held dear.

The Indians had soon hewed away a part of the door, so that they could force themselves in, one by one, but not very rapidly. This slow mode of entrance gave time to Mrs. M. to despatch them with an axe, and drag them in; so that before those without were aware of the fate of those inside, she had, with a little assistance from her husband, formed quite a pile of dead bodies within and around the door; and even the little children, half dead though they at first were with fear, had gradually begun to recover from their fright.

The Indians, finding their party so rapidly disappearing, at length began to suspect what was their fate, and accordingly gave up their efforts in that direction. They now attempted to descend into the house by way of the chimney. The united wisdom and presence of mind of the family was again put in requisition, and they emptied upon the fire the contents of a feather bed, which brought down, half smothered, those Indians that were in the chimney, who were also soon and easily despatched. The remainder of the party, now very much reduced in numbers, became quite discouraged, and concluded it was best to retire.

I have not related this story because I suppose any of my readers will ever be tried in this particular manner. Many of them, however, may be placed in circumstances exceedingly trying; and their lives and those of others may depend on a little presence of mind.

Suppose, now, that Mrs. M., instead of dragging her wounded husband into the house and fastening the door, had stood still and screamed; or suppose she had fainted, or run away; what would have been the result? We do not know, it is true; but we know enough of the Indian mode of warfare to see that no condition could well be more perilous.

It cannot be denied that the large share of nervous sensibility which is allotted to the female constitution, peculiarly unfits woman for scenes of blood, like that to which I have alluded. And yet we see what can be done, as a last resort. [Footnote: Some persons object to the detail or such a scene of murder as this, even as an illustration of an important principle. They dislike to present such things to the youthful mind; and so do I. But it should be remembered that this book is not for mere children, but rather for young women; and is therefore less objectionable than if it were written for persons much younger.]

But if most females were fitted for trying emergencies, as I doubt not they could be, how much better they could meet the more common accidents and dangers to which human existence is daily more or less liable. And ought they not to be thus fitted?

Do you ask how item be done? This is precisely the question I should expect would be asked by those who have a strong desire for improvement. It is a work that is at present chiefly left undone, both by parents and teachers, and yet hundreds of lives are lost every year for the want of it; and hundreds of others are likely to be lost in the same way every year for many years to come, unless the work is taken up as a work of importance, and studied with as much zeal as grammar, or geography, or botany, or mathematics.

It is a most pitiable sight to see a young woman, twelve, fifteen, or it may be eighteen years of age, left to take care of a babe, suffer its clothes to get on fire by some accident, and then, without the least particle of self-command, only jump up and down and scream, till the child is burnt to death; or what perhaps is still worse, rush out for relief, leaving the door wide open to let through a current of air to hasten the work of destruction.

Equally distressing and pitiable is it, to see females, young or old, losing all presence of mind the moment a horse takes fright, or a gale of wind capsizes the vessel in which they are travelling, and by their erratic movements, depriving themselves of the only opportunity which remains to them, of saving themselves or of assisting to save others.

But the question recurs—How can these evils be prevented? In what way can our young women be taught—or in what way can they be induced to teach themselves—the important art of commanding themselves, on all occasions, and in all emergencies?

An aged but excellent minister of the gospel with whom I had the honor and the pleasure of being intimately acquainted, once said, that the only way of being prepared for the sudden accidents of life—by being able to keep cool and possess our souls in peace—was to think on the subject often, and consider what we would do, should such and such accidents occur.

Thus we should consider often what we ought to do, if a horse in a carriage should run away with us; if we should awake and find the house on fire over our heads—what to be done, if we were in this room or in that, &c.; if our clothes should take fire; if we should be burnt or scalded—what to be done, if scalded with water, and what, if with milk, oil, or any other substance; [Footnote: A very small portion of chemical knowledge is sufficient to teach any person that the falling of a quantity of boiling oil or fat on any part of the body, will cause a deeper and more dangerous burn, than the same quantity of boiling water applied in the same manner; and consequently, will require very different treatment. Water boils at

212 degrees of Fahrenheit; oil at about 600.—I have entered minutely into this subject in my work entitled "The Mother in her Family" chapters xxiv. xxv. and xxvi] if a child should fall into a well, be kicked by a horse, be seized by convulsions, or break or dislocate a limb, &c.

It will be asked, I know, of what avail it is to think over and over what should be done, without the instructions, either of experience or science. But we can have these instructions, to some extent, whenever we seek after them. The great trouble is, we are not in the habit of seeking for them; and what we do not seek, we rarely, if ever, find.

There are around every young woman, those whose judgment is worth something in this matter. It is not always the old—though it is more generally such. There are those who live in the world almost half a century without learning any thing; and there are also those who become wise in a quarter of a century. The wise, whatever may be their age, are the persons for you to consult; and the older such persons are, the better—because the greater is likely to be their wisdom. The truly wise, are always growing wiser; it is the fool alone who remains stationary. Wise and observing friends will probably tell you—or at least relate anecdotes to you, from which you may gather the conclusion—that when the clothes of a child have caught fire, you may often smother the flame by wrapping him instantly in a thick woollen blanket:—that it is seldom entirely safe to open the doors into an adjoining room—at least without great caution—when the house which we are in is discovered to be on fire; but the best way, as a general rule, is, to escape by the scuttle, if there be one, or by a ladder, or by letting ourselves down to the ground, if the distance is not too great, through the windows. This last is often the best way, though not always the most expeditious one. Many sleep with a rope in their bed-rooms to tie to the bed-post, as a means of letting themselves down, should there be occasion; while others rely on the bed-clothes—to make a rope of them by tying several articles together.

But it was no part of my purpose, in this work, to direct to the appropriate methods of saving ourselves or our friends from harm, in case of accidents or emergencies; but only to point to the subject, and leave the reader to pursue it. The intelligent young woman who sets about gaining the habit of self-command, will not only consult the experience of others, but observe, and reflect, and reason on the case, herself. She will often originate plans and means of escape, in places and, circumstances of danger, which she would not gain from others in a hundred or a thousand years.

There is one other means of improvement in the art of self-command, on which I do not know that any writer on the subject has dwelt with much earnestness. And yet it is as plain and simple as can be. It is to make the most of every little accident or emergency that actually overtakes or surprises us. I know from personal experience, that a great deal may be done in this way. There are those who, though they were formerly frightened half out of their senses, at the sudden sight of a harmless snake, have brought themselves, by dint of long effort, to so much presence of mind, as only to start a little at first—and to be as calm, and composed, and self-possessed, in a few seconds afterward, as if nothing had happened. And the same presence of mind may be obtained in other surprises or emergencies. Besides, she who is learning to command herself at sight of a snake or a dog; is at the same time acquiring the power to command herself in any other circumstances where self-command may be necessary.

I wish the principle indicated by the last statement were more generally perceived. I wish it were distinctly understood, that what we want is, to gain the habit of self-command in all circumstances, rather than to be able to work ourselves up to a proper state of feeling in particular cases; and that this habit is to be acquired by frequent familiar conversation on the subject, and by daily practice in the continually recurring small matters of life. It is, indeed, in governing ourselves in these small matters—which recur so frequently, and are regarded as so trifling as to have not only no moral character in themselves, but no influence in the formation of character—that the art to which I am now directing your attention, is to be chiefly acquired. They who defer the work till some larger or more striking emergency arrives, will not be likely to make much progress; for they begin at the wrong end of the matter. They begin exactly where they ought to end.

CHAPTER IX.

DECISION OF CHARACTER.

Decision of character as important to young women as to others. Why it is so. Illustration of the subject by a Scripture anecdote. Misery and danger of indecision. How to reform. Perseverance. Errors of modern education.

This trait of character has been recommended to young men too exclusively. I know of no reason why it is not equally important to young women, and equally becoming the sex in general. One thing, at any rate, I do know; which is, that thousands of young women—and the world through their imperfection—suffer, in no trifling degree, from the want of this virtue.

I call it a *virtue*. What is there that produces more evil—directly or indirectly—than the want of power, when occasion requires it, to say YES, or NO? As long as with half the human race—and the more influential half, too-*no* does not mean *no,* and *yes* does not mean *yes,* there will be a vast amount of vice, and crime, and suffering in the world, as the natural consequence. And is not that which is the cause of so much evil, nearly akin to vice? And is any thing more entitled to the name of virtue, than its opposite?

Let me illustrate my meaning by a Scripture example. When Balak, the king of Moab, undertook to extort a curse upon Israel, from Balaam, the latter did not say *no*; but only said, the Lord would not permit him to do what was required. He left neither to Balak nor to his messengers, any reason to conclude that his virtue was invulnerable. On the contrary, as the event plainly shows, his answer was just such a one as encouraged them to prosecute their attempts to seduce him.

Now it is precisely this sort of refusal, direct or implied, in a thousand cases which might be named, which brings down evil, not only upon those who make it, but upon others. They mean *no*, perhaps; and yet it is not certain that the decision is—like the laws of the Medea and Persians—irrevocable. Something in the tone, or manner, or both combined, leaves room to hope for success in time to come. "The woman who deliberates, is lost," we are told: and is it not so? Do not many who say *no* with hesitancy, still retain the power and the disposition to deliberate? And is it not so understood?

It is—I repeat it—a great misfortune—a very great one—not to know how and when to say NO. Indeed, the undecided are more than unfortunate; they are very unsafe. They who cannot say *no*, are never their own keepers; they are always, more or less, in the power and at the command of others. They may form a thousand resolutions a day, to withstand in the hour of temptation; and yet, if the temptation comes, and they have not acquired decision of character, it is ten to one but they will yield to it.

Is it too much to say, that half the world are miserable on this account,—miserable themselves, and a source of misery to others? Is it too much to say, that decision of character is more important to young women than to any other class of persons whatever?

But as it is in every thing or almost every thing else, so it is in this matter: they who would reform themselves, must begin with the smaller matters of life. The great trials—those of decision no less than those of other traits of human character—come but seldom; and they who allow themselves, habitually, to vacillate, and hesitate, and remain undecided, in the every-day concerns of life, will inevitably do so in those larger matters which recur less frequently.

No one will succeed in acquiring true decision of character, without perseverance. A few feeble efforts, continued a day or two, or a week, are by no means sufficient to change the character or form the habit. The efforts must be earnest, energetic, and unremitted; and must be persevered in through life.

I am not ignorant that many philosophers and physiologists have denied that woman possesses the power of perseverance in what she undertakes, in any eminent degree. A British writer, distinguished for his boldness, if not for his metaphysical acuteness, maintains with much earnestness, that woman, by her vital organization, is much wanting in perseverance. This notion may or may not be true. Certain it is, however, that she has her peculiarities, as well as man his. But whether she has little or much native power of perseverance in what she undertakes, is not so important a question, as whether she makes a proper use of the power she possesses.

> "Who does the best his circumstance allows,
> Does well; acts nobly: angels could no more."

We are required, however, to do that best which "circumstance" does allow, as much as is the highest seraph; and woman is not the less bound to persevere in matters where perseverance would become her, because her native power of perseverance is feeble, if indeed it is so. On the contrary, this very fact makes the duty of perseverance to the utmost extent of the means God has put into her hands, the more urgent— especially as *small powers* are apt to be overlooked.

There is one habit which should be cultivated, not only for its usefulness in general, but especially for its value in leading to true decision of character. I mean, the habit of doing every thing which it devolves upon us to do at all, precisely *at the time* when it ought to be done. Every thing in human character goes to wreck, under the reign of procrastination, while prompt action gives to all things a corresponding and proportional life and energy. Above all, every thing in the shape of decision of character is lost by delay. It should be a sacred rule with every individual who lives in the world for any higher purpose than merely to live, never to put off, for a single moment, a thing which ought to be done immediately—if it be no more than the cleaning or changing of a garment.

When I see a young woman neglecting, from day to day, her correspondents—her pile of letters constantly increasing, and her dread of putting pen and thoughts to paper accumulating as rapidly—I never fail to conclude, at once, that whatever other excellent qualities she may possess, she is a stranger to the one in question. She who cannot make up her mind to answer a letter when she knows it ought to be answered—and in general a letter ought to be answered soon after it is received—will not be likely to manifest decision in other things of still greater importance. The same is true, as I have said already several times, in regard to indecision in other things of even less moment than the writing of a letter. It is manifest especially in regard to the matter of rising in the morning. She who knows it is time to get up, and yet cannot decide to do so, and consequently lies yawning a little longer, "and yet a little longer still," can never, I am bold to say, while this indolence and indecision are indulged, be decided in any thing else—at least; habitually.

She may, indeed, be so by fits and starts; but the habit will never be so confirmed as to be regarded as an essential element of her character.

Nearly all the habits of modern female education—I mean the *fashionable* education of the family and school—are entirely at war with the virtue I am endeavoring to inculcate. It would be a miracle, almost, if a young woman who has been educated in a fashionable family, under the eye of a fashionable mother, and at a fashionable boarding school, under the direction of a teacher whose main object is to please her patrons, should come out to the world, without being quite destitute of all true decision of character. If it were the leading object of our boarding schools to form the habit of indecision, they could not succeed better than many of them now do. They furnish to the world a set of beings who are any thing but what the world wants, and who are more likely to do almost any thing else, than to be the means of reforming it.

CHAPTER X

SELF-DEPENDENCE.

Fashionable education. Why there is so little self-dependence in the world. Why orphans sometimes make out well in the world. Error corrected. What young women once were. What they are now. The best character formed under difficulties. Cause of the present helpless condition of females. Three or four to get breakfast. Modes of breaking up these habits. Anecdote of an independent young woman. Appeal to the reader.

Here, again, our fashionable modes of education are wrong; and here, too, almost every young woman who is determined on improvement, has a great work to perform.

It is one of the most difficult things in the world—perhaps it is one of the impossibles—to bring up children amid comforts and conveniences, and yet at the same time to cultivate in them the habit of self-dependence—or, as some would call it, the habit of independence.

And yet nothing is more true, than that human character has always, with few if any exceptions, been most fully developed and most harmoniously and healthfully formed, amid difficulties. Mr. M'Clure, the distinguished geologist, whose opportunities for observation in the world have been very great, says that orphans, as a general rule, make their way best in the world. Without claiming for myself so many years of observation, by thirty or forty, as this distinguished veteran in natural science, I should be glad to make one modification of his conclusion, before adopting it as my own. I would say, that the misfortune of having no parents at all, is scarcely greater than that of having over-indulgent ones; and that the number of those who are spoiled by indulgence, is greater than the number of those who are spoiled by being made orphans.

It cannot be that an institution ordained by Heaven as one of its first laws, should so completely fail in accomplishing its design—that of blessing mankind—as Mr. M'Clure represents. It cannot be that parents, as a general rule, are a misfortune. Such a belief is greatly erroneous.

The truth is, that when we look about us and see so many spoiled, who appear to be well bred, our attention is so exclusively directed to these strange, but, in a dense population, frequently occurring cases, that we begin, ere long, to fancy the exception to be the general rule. And again, when we see here and there an orphan—and in a population like ours, quite a multitude in the aggregate—making her way well in the world, we are liable to make another wrong conclusion, and to say that her success belongs to the general rule, when it is only an exception to it.

Nevertheless—and I have no wish to conceal the fact—it is extremely difficult, if not dangerous, to attempt to form good and useful character in the lap of ease and indulgence. There needs privation and hard struggle, to develope the soul and the body. Even Zion, the city of our God, is represented in Scripture as recruiting her inhabitants only by throes and agonies.

Let it not be thought, then, that our young women in New England—a land of comparative ease, quiet and affluence—can be brought up as they ought to be, without much pains-taking. A century ago, things were, in this respect, more favorable. Then there were struggles; and these were the means of forming a race of men and women, of whom the world might have been proud. Then the young women knew how to take care of themselves; and having been taught how to take care of themselves, they knew how to take care of others.

But "times are altered." Thousands of young women—and the same is true of young men—are trained from the very cradle, scarcely to know any thing of want or difficulty. All is comparative ease, and comfort, and quiet around them; and they are led by ease and indulgence to love to have it so. They are trained, as I have elsewhere said, to depend on the world and its inhabitants for their happiness—not to originate happiness and diffuse it. They are trained, in effect, to believe that happiness, or blessedness, consists—contrary to the saying of our Lord and Saviour—in *receiving*; not in *giving*.

The time *was*, I say once more, when most young women, if thrown by the hard hand of necessity upon their own resources, could yet take care of themselves. No matter how great their poverty or affliction— how large or how deep their cup of adversity or trial—they would, in general, struggle through it, and come out as gold seven times refined. Mothers left with large families of helpless children, and with no means of sustaining them but the labor of their own hands, and daughters left without either parent, would wind their way along in the world, and the world be both the wiser and the better for their influence.

Now, on the contrary, mothers and young women left destitute, are apt to be, of all beings, except the merest infants of the former, the most helpless.

This applies to even a large portion of what are called the poor. In reality, however, we have no poor—or next to none. Our very paupers are comparatively rich. They dress, and eat, and drink, and *dwell* like princes. How, then, can they be so very poor?

It is true, that nearly all of our young women are trained to something in the shape of labor. Very few, indeed, are trained to positive indolence. But what is their labor, generally speaking? A little sewing, or knitting, or embroidery; or still worse, in circumstances of poverty or peculiar necessity, a life of spinning, or weaving, or braiding; or some other mechanical occupation which has no tendency to prepare them for true self-dependence.

I have said we have little poverty existing among us. Is it not so? Is not the life of young women in the great mass of our New England families, very far removed from any feeling of want or suffering?

But though not trained in real indigence, they might be trained to self-dependence. They might be, and always ought to be, trained to make their own beds; make and mend their own garments; make bread; and, in fact, to attend to the whole usual routine of duties involved in the care of themselves and a family. But is it so? Are not all these things done, to a vast extent, either by servants, hired girls, or the mother? And if the mother employs her daughters in assisting her, is it not apt to be just so far as is *convenient to herself*, and no farther? In short, who can often find the individual mother or daughter, who considers hard work, and care, and obstacles, and difficulties—such as all the world acknowledge are required in order to form good and useful character—as any thing but task work and drudgery—a curse, and not a blessing, to mankind?

True it is—and greatly to be lamented—that many of our young women are not well able, for want of physical vigor and energy, to encounter poverty, and hardship, and obstacles, and suffering. But this deteriorated condition of female character in New England, is owing, in no small degree, to the very kind of education—miseducation, rather—of which I am now complaining. Would mothers do their duty— could they do it, I mean, in the midst of abundance—the state of things would be very much altered for the better.

It is not uncommon in the schools of Europe, especially the female schools, to assign to each older pupil the care of some younger one, for whom she is more or less responsible, particularly as to behaviour. This leads, in no small degree, to self-effort and self-dependence; and might be practised in families as well as in schools, with equally good effects.

But there is another course which is better still, in many respects. It is not unusual in our New England families, where there are several daughters, when they are employed at all—I mean about household concerns—to have them all employed at the same thing at once. Thus, if breakfast is to be prepared, all are to engage in it. One goes this way, another that, and another that; and it sometimes happens that they cross each other's path and come into actual conflict. One goes for one thing, another for another, and so on; and it is not uncommon for two or three to go for the same article.

That three or four females may thus spend all their time for an hour or more in getting breakfast, when one alone would do it much more quietly and a great deal better, and in little more time than is occupied by the whole of them, is not the worst of the evil. The great trouble is, that no one is acquiring the habit of self-dependence. On the contrary, they are acquiring so strong a habit of doing things in company, that they hardly know how to do them otherwise. True, there is pleasure connected with this sort of dependence—and most persons are exceedingly fond of it; but the question is whether it is useful—and not whether it is or is not pleasurable.

Is it best for young women to become so much accustomed to *assist*, merely, in cooking, and in performing other household offices, as to feel, even at thirty years of age, as if they could do nothing without the aid of others?

I hardly know what a young woman is to do, who finds herself in the dependent condition of which I have been speaking. The habit is not very likely to be broken, so long as she remains in the place where it was formed. I have, however, seen such a habit successfully broken up; in one instance; and perhaps it may be useful to relate it.

A young friend and neighbor of mine, in a family where there were several young men of nearly the same age, happening to find out the evil of doing the smaller work of the morning and evening in this company manner—that what was "every body's business," in the language of a common maxim, "was nobody's"— resolved on a change. He accordingly proposed to his companions to take turns in doing the work. One was to do it faithfully—the whole of it—for a month; another for the next month; and so on. The plan succeeded most admirably. Each became accustomed to a degree of responsibility; and each began to acquire the habit of doing things independently, without the aid of a dozen others.

Perhaps this method might be generally introduced into families, as it has already been, in substance, into some of our boarding schools. It is at least worth while for a young woman who perceives her need of such an arrangement, to attempt it. To be suddenly required to make a batch of bread, or wash the garments, or cook the victuals of a household, and to feel, at twenty years of age, utterly at a loss how to perform the whole routine of these familiar household duties, must be both distressing to herself and painful to others.

Of course it is not desirable to see our young women all orphans, and brought up as domestics, for the sake of having them brought up in such a way as to be good for something, [Footnote: Nor can I wish to see young women trained to do the "buying and selling," instead of men, in order to give energy to their character; although I do not doubt that such a course is often successful. It is related by Mr. Ennis, a highly credible traveller that in Bali and Lombok, two islands lying eastward of Java, the females do all the buying and selling, even to the amount of thousands of dollars. "This probably gives" he says, "to the whole race of people a portion of that boldness and energy for which they are a little distinguished." But then, as he very honestly adds, it gives the women somewhat of a masculine character—a thing which should not by any means be encouraged.] instead of being the poor dependent beings they too commonly are; yet it were greatly to be desired, that without the disadvantages of orphans at service in families, they could have the energy and self-dependence of such persons.

Allow me to relate, for your instruction, a few anecdotes respecting an individual, who was, to all intents and purposes, an orphan, but who was, nevertheless, more useful in life, and more truly happy, than a hundred or a thousand of some of those passive mortals who float through life on the streams of abundance, without feeling the agitation of tide or current, and only discover the misery of such a course when they fall into the gulf of insignificance.

This individual had been abandoned by one of her parents very early in life, and had been also early separated by poverty from the other. She had lived in various families, and had been compelled to hard labor, and sometimes to menial services. At length she married a person as poor as herself, though not so independent. He had been bred in the midst of ease; and was, consequently, indolent. But she was determined on "going ahead" in the world; and her ambition at length roused her husband.

The latter now engaged in hard labor, by the day or the month, among his neighbors; while the wife took care of the concerns at home. This continued for fifteen or sixteen years, before their joint labors procured land enough for the husband to work on, at home. In the mean time, however, they had a number of children; and the mother's cares and labors of course increased. For several of the first of these years, the husband was seldom at home to assist or encourage her, in the summer, except during the Sabbath and occasionally at evening; so that though this diminished the labor of cooking, it left her with her children wholly on her hands, and a great deal of unavoidable labor, such as washing and ironing. The latter work she did for her husband, as well as for her children and herself: and it was therefore an item of considerable moment—especially as she was obliged to bring water for this and all her domestic purposes in pails, the distance of twenty-five or thirty rods, a part of the year, and of ten rods or so, the other part; besides which, she had to pick up much of her wood, for the six summer months, in the woods nearly a quarter of a mile distant, carry it home in her arms, and to cut it for the fire-place. Added to all this, was the labor of *brewing* once or twice a week; for in those days, when poverty denied cider to a family, the beer barrel was regarded as indispensable.

Nor were her domestic concerns, properly so called, her only labors. She spun and wove cloth for the use of her family, besides weaving for some of her neighbors. She also spun and wove a great deal of coarse cloth, at shares; and thus purchased a large part of the smaller necessaries of the family, and not a little of the clothing.

She continued this course, I say, something like fifteen years. Never, to my knowledge, unless she was actually sick, did she receive any assistance in her labors—not so much as a day's work of washing. And yet under all these disadvantages, she reared—almost without help even from the children themselves, as the difference between the oldest and the youngest was only about eight years—a family of four children.

I have sometimes wondered how she accomplished so much, by her own unaided efforts. But the whole secret lay in her power of self-dependence. She could do every thing alone. She had been trained to it. She was truly independent; as much so, perhaps, as a female can be in this world.

I might have added, that notwithstanding these incessant labors, I have often known her walk four or five miles to church on the Sabbath, and home again in the same manner; that she was neat and orderly; and that she found much time to read and converse with her children, and for social visiting.

Reader, I do not ask you to imitate this veteran matron; for it would be too much to ask of any individual in any age, especially the present. But I ask you, and with great earnestness, to acquire the power of self-dependence—and to do it immediately. Make it a matter of conscience. Bear constantly in mind, that whatever *has* been done, *may* be done. Shame on those who, knowing the value of self-dependence, and having the power to acquire it, pass through life so shiftless, that they cannot do the least thing without aid—the aid of a host of relatives or menials. It is quite time that woman should understand her power and her strength, and govern herself accordingly. It is quite time for her to stand upright in her native, heaven-born dignity, and show to the world—and to angels, even, as well as to men—for what woman was made, and wherein, consists her true excellence.

CHAPTER XI.

REASONING AND ORIGINALITY

Females not expected to be reasoners. Effects of modern education on the reasoning powers. Education of former days, illustrated by an anecdote of as octogenarian. Extracts from her correspondence. Difficulty in getting the ears of mankind. The reasoning powers in man susceptible of cultivation indefinitely. Reflections on the importance of maternal effort and female education.

I know not why a young woman should not reason correctly as well as a young man. And yet I must confess that, some how or other, a masculine seems to be often attached to the thought of strong reasoning powers in the female sex. To say of such or such a young woman, She is a bold and powerful reasoner—would it not be a little uncommon? Would it be received as a compliment? Would it not be regarded as a little out of the way—and, to coin a term, as rather unfeminine?

Perhaps the habit of boldly tracing effects up to their causes, and of reasoning upon them, is a little more uncommon among the young misses of our boarding schools and our more fashionable families, both of city and country, than among those of the plainer sort of people. Certain it is, at all events, that the former would be regarded as reasoning persons with much more reluctance than the latter. And yet the former has probably been taught mathematics, and all those sciences which are supposed to develope and strengthen the mental faculties, and give energy to the reasoning powers.

For myself, I have many doubts whether we are really—whether the sex themselves are, I mean—so much the gainers by the superficial knowledge of modern days, which tends to the exclusion, in the result, of that good old fashioned education to house-work, which was given by the mothers of New England, in the days of her primitive beauty and glory. Then were our young women, for the times, reasoning women; then were they good for something. A few of those precious relics of a comparatively golden age, have come down nearly to our own times. I have even seen several of them since the beginning of the nineteenth century. There is one of this description, more than eighty years of age, now living with a son of hers in one of the Middle States. Her sphere of action, however, in the days of her activity, lay not there, but on one of those delightful hills which are found at the termination of the Green Mountain range, in New England. There, in her secluded country residence, among plain people, and with only plain means, with her husband absent much of the time, she educated—not instructed, merely, nor brought up at school, but educated—a large family of children, most of whom live to bless her memory and the world. So devoted was this woman to her household duties, and to the right education of her family, that for eleven of the first and *hardest* years of her life, she never for once left the hill on which she dwelt—a mile or so in extent.

And yet this female was a woman of reasoning powers superior to those of most men. She understood, thoroughly, every ordinary topic of conversation, and could discuss well any subject which came within her grasp. She has been for a few years past, one of my most regular and most valued correspondents; and nothing but her great age and great reluctance to put pen to paper, would, I presume, prevent her from writing more frequently than she is accustomed to do. As a specimen of her style, I venture to insert a paragraph or two from her letters. The first was written when she was in her eightieth year.

"I am glad to find you in the enjoyment of health—able to be busily and usefully employed for this and coming generations. I would like, if it was God's will, to be usefully employed in *such* ways, too; but though I am so greatly favored as to be able to *think* as well as ever, I cannot work with my wonted facility and despatch. I cannot 'labor with my hands,' so as to have 'to give to him that needeth,' because my hands are weak and lame. Once I could fill six sheets of letter paper in a day, without weariness; but now, if I can fill this sheet, decently, in *two* days, I am ready to boast of it, as an achievement. When I look back and see my former activity, I wonder if that *was myself*, and am almost ready to doubt my identity. But every thing in its course; first rising into life, then decaying. The world itself is not to stand forever; and of course the things animate and inanimate which are upon it, must partake of its transitoriness."

Again, when she was within a few weeks of eighty years of age, (which was in January, 1838,) she wrote to me in the following vein of playfulness:

"As I can invent nothing new, I must utter such truisms as I have picked up by the way, in almost eighty years; for you say to me, *write*—and of course I obey, and scribble on. Now I say to *you*—and may I say it to Mrs. A. too?—WRITE. Write very sensibly, by the way; for old as I am, I am a sharp critic. I read in my early days Lord Kaimes' Elements, and I have been working up these elements ever since; and if I cannot *invent*, I can understand what is fairly presented to me: so you will receive this as a caution. But don't be afraid! I'll tell you another thing, of which perhaps you are not aware: I had rather have one letter warm from the heart, than a dozen from the head."

"I was delighted to think you were pleased with my philosophy—for I never dreamed I uttered any. As to my politics, I was pretty well drilled in the school of Washington, after seeing through the revolutionary struggle; and that was no mean school, I assure you. Washington was a statesman! I see but *few* now; but when I do see one, I make him my best courtesy. And as to my theology, I learned that from the pilgrim fathers."

Now whether those of my younger readers of a new generation, who, perhaps, almost despise both letter writing and reasoning,—whether any of these, I say, will see either form or comeliness—any thing inviting—in these paragraphs, I cannot say. But I can tell them, at once, that *I* do; and it sometimes seems to me, that no greater human benefaction could be offered to mankind, than the application of those principles and methods of female education, in family and school, which would produce such minds and bodies as those of which we have, in the case of this aged woman, an example!

Perhaps, however, it is almost useless to hope for better times, at present, for reasons, among others, which are given in another place by my aged correspondent. "The mischief now-a-days," she says, "is, that every one is on a railroad, impelled by steam power, and cannot stop; so all speak at once, and none hear. What a state is this! But it is true of the world in general. I see but few who are self-possessed. I wonder when I see any one who is so; and I wonder if I am so myself."

But we are not only unwilling to stay to hear—we are unwilling to stay to teach. It would be no hard matter for parents and teachers—especially by beginning early—to establish in the young of both sexes, habits of right reasoning. I am afraid, however, that parents and teachers themselves do not perceive the value of such a habit, and that they are not likely to do so for some time to come.

All, however, which remains for me to do, I must do. This is, to press upon the few whose ear I can gain, the importance of this part of self-education. Do not despise the idea of reasoning on subjects which come before you; nor think it masculine or old fashioned. Not only accustom yourselves to reason, but to reason on every thing. There is almost as great a difference between a young woman who takes all things upon trust, scarcely knowing that she can use her own powers in the investigation of truth, and one who has been, like my worthy and venerable correspondent, in the habit of observing and reasoning seventy or eighty years, as there is between a Sam Patch and a Bowditch—or a Hottentot and a Newton. Would that our young women knew this, and would conduct themselves accordingly!

There is nothing in the wide field of human improvement which better repays the labor of cultivation, than the reasoning powers. Nor is there any thing which does more to perfect and adorn the human being. With the highest and noblest rational powers, the human family—especially the female part of it—seems to me to accomplish least happily the great work for which they were created, than any other earthly existences. The little all of knowledge which pertains to the lower animals, "flows in at once," says Dr. Young; whereas, "were man to live coeval with the sun, the patriarch pupil might be learning still, yet dying, leave his lessons half unlearnt." And yet the former fill, happily, the sphere which God in nature assigned them; while the latter, with all his capacities and powers of reason, conscience, &c., wanders incessantly from his orbit, and must be a most unsightly spectacle to God and holy angels, and all other high and noble intelligences. When will man return to his native sphere, and the moral and intellectual world move in due harmony and happiness, like the physical? When will each moral creation of the Divine Architect, move round its great spiritual centre, with the same beauty, and majesty, and glory, which is manifest in the motions of the physical world? Never, I am sure, till mothers and teachers, who are, as it seems, the authors alike of human happiness and human misery, come up to their appropriate work; and never will there be such mothers, till young women are better trained. And the latter will never be better trained, till the work of education, especially of self-education, is undertaken with much better views of its objects and ends, and with a thousand times more earnestness and perseverance, and I might even say *enthusiasm*, than has as yet been manifested.

CHAPTER XII.

INVENTION.

Why woman has invented so few thing. Abundant room for the exercise of her inventive powers. Hints. Particular need of a reform in cookery. Appeal to young women on this subject.

Is it not strange, that in a world where have been sought out—time immemorial—so many inventions, so few should as yet have been originated by woman?

What have the inventive powers of woman accomplished, even within what have been usually regarded as her own precincts? Has she invented many special improvements in the art of house-keeping? Have the labors of knitting, sewing, making, mending, washing, cooking, &c., been materially facilitated, or rendered more effective, by her ingenuity? Has she done much to advance the important art of bread-making towards perfection?

Why has she not done more? Is genius confined to our sex? Nay, is there even no common ingenuity out of the range of our own walks? Has not the young woman, when she begins the world, the same mental faculties, in number and kind, with the young man? How happens it, then, that the world is filled with inventions, and so few of them originated by woman?

There is a wide range for improvement in that department of human labor which has usually been confined to the female sex—especially in the department of *infant education*. Nor is there any department in which invention would tell with so much efficiency in the cause of human happiness, as in that. Let our young women consider this; and let them resolve on inventing something in their oven particular sphere, which shall turn to the general account.

When I speak of the appropriate sphere of woman, and of her taxing her powers of invention there, I would by no means indulge myself in any narrow or circumscribed views in regard to her field of operation. I should have no sort of objection to the application of her inventive powers to the work of facilitating the usual labors of the other sex—particularly in the departments of agriculture and horticulture.

But I do not perceive any necessity for this. I believe there is work enough—profitable and philanthropic work, too—to task woman's powers of invention for many centuries, without her going out of her appropriate sphere. In the art of cookery especially—which certainly has a great deal to do with physical education and physical improvement—there is great room for the exercise of her inventive powers. This important art is, as yet, entirely in its infancy; and where any progress has been made, it has been chiefly in a wrong direction, and under the guidance of wrong principles. Be it yours, young women, to give this matter a right direction, and to bring it to bear as efficiently on the happiness of mankind, as it has hitherto on their slow destruction.

CHAPTER XIII.

OBSERVATION AND REFLECTION.

Advice of Dr. Dwight. Other counsels to the young. Some persons of both sexes are always seeing, but never reflecting. An object deserving of pity. Zimmerman's views. Reading to get rid of reflection. Worse things still.

"Keep your eyes open," was the reiterated counsel of a distinguished theologian, of this country—the late Dr. Timothy Dwight—to a young student of his; and it was, in the main, very wholesome advice. And in so far as it is wholesome for young men, I do not see but it is equally so for young women.

"Your countenance open, your thoughts close, you will go safe through the world"—was the advice of another individual, of less eminence, to a young friend of his; and did it not savor a little too much of selfishness, and perhaps of concealment, it would, like the advice of Dr. Dwight, be worthy of careful consideration. It does not partake quite enough of the gospel spirit and sentiment—"As a man hath received, so let him give." It encourages us to get wisdom, but not to communicate it.

I have said that the advice of Dr. Dwight was, in the main, wholesome. The only objection that can be made to it is, that it gives no encouragement to reflection. Some may suppose it to mean, that observation, or *seeing*, is every thing. Now there are those who appear to see too much. They *always* have their eyes open. They are never satisfied otherwise. They absolutely hate all reflection.

Of this description of persons—I am sorry to say it—our young women furnish a full proportion. Not a very small number of the female sex are so educated, that it is quite painful for them to turn the current of their thoughts inward:—they will do almost any thing in the world, not absolutely criminal, to prevent it. It cannot, indeed, be quite said, that they observe too much; but it is perfectly safe to say, that they see too much. If they should see much less with their eyes, and the soul were left to its own reflections, the result would be, no doubt, exceedingly happy. Solitude is as necessary as action; and to both sexes.

No person is more pitiable than the individual of either sex—and such individuals are by no means scarce in our own-who cannot be easy unless perpetually running to see some new sight, or, like the Athenians of old, to hear or to tell some new thing; who is no where so happy as when in company, and no where so miserable as when alone.

Zimmerman, in his work on Solitude—a pleasant book, by the way, notwithstanding its gloomy name—has some very appropriate and useful remarks on the advantages of being by ourselves a part of the time, as a means of improvement. Should any of my young readers be sorely afflicted with the disease I have just mentioned-a dread of themselves, or of their own thoughts, rather—I beg them to read Zimmerman. But read him, if you read him at all, very thoroughly.

Some persons read solely to get rid of reflection. Worse than this, even; some persons read, work and play—and I had almost said, go to church, and put themselves in the attitude of prayer and praise—to get rid of themselves and their reflections. Who will show us any good thing? is their constant cry: not, Who will lead us, by external agencies, or by any other means, to sound and useful reflection. Who will show us ourselves? is a cry which, among the young women of New England, as well as those of most other countries, is too seldom heard.

The best advice I can give to such persons—next to that given in the Sermon on the Mount, where they are directed to enter into their closet—is, to read with great care, or rather to study, Watts on the Improvement of the Mind. That is a work which has probably done as much good in the way of which I am now speaking, as any book—the Bible excepted—in the English language.

CHAPTER XIV.

DETRACTION AND SCANDAL.

Universal prevalence of detraction and slander. Proofs Shakspeare. Burns the poet. Self-knowledge, how much to be desired. Reference to the work of Mrs. Opie—to our own hearts—to the Bible.

Let it not be supposed, for one moment, that I consider young women as more generally in the habit of detraction than other people; for I venture on no comparisons of the kind. All I presume to take for granted is, that they are often exceedingly faulty in this respect, and need counsel and caution. Were there any doubts on the latter point, one would think they might very readily be removed by reading the excellent work of Amelia Opie, entitled, "Detraction Displayed; or, a Cure for Scandal."

This detraction or scandal is so common every where in life, that multitudes are addicted to it without the shadow of a suspicion that they are so. Thousands and thousands of young women whose hearts would recoil at the bare recital of deeds of butchery and blood—nay, who would faint at the sight of the severities, not to say cruelties, which, under the guise of parental discipline, or on the plea of authority, are often and hourly inflicted on the bodies of young and old—who will yet rob and murder their unoffending neighbors. For there is no little truth in what Shakspeare says so pungently—

"Who steals my purse, steals trash; 'tis something, nothing;
'Twas mine, 't is his, it may be slave to thousands:
But he that filches from me my good name,
Robs me of that which not enriches him,
And makes me poor indeed."

Nor is there less of truth in what the evangelist says, that "whoso hateth his brother" (and does not a slanderer *hate*?) "is a murderer."

I know it may seem harsh to fasten on any class of the community, and above all, on the young of either sex, the charge of robbery or murder. But is it not proper that the truth should be told? And if there is such a propensity in us to competition in its varied forms, that not only thoughts but words of detraction are, as it were, forever on our thoughtless tongues and lips, and we will not, though often warned, set a guard over the latter, is it not right that we should be represented as the robbers of reputation? And if there is such a disposition to try to be first in the community, and to compel those around us to take the second place—the lower seat—as generates envy and hatred—the *seeds* of murder—is it not right to warn the young of their danger? And when we find them callous to our representations of the truth—when we find their hearts almost as unmoved as the firm rocks they tread on, notwithstanding our most faithful exhibitions of human depravity, as is evinced by the slander, the detraction and the calumny which every where prevail, and which many must see, as in a glass, to prevail in their own bosoms, while yet their very blood recoils at the tales of imaginary wo from the pen of Bulwer, or some other novelist of kindred fame—is it not proper to remind people of what the evangelist says of hatred, that it is murder?

Burns, the poet, sought some power who would bestow on us the gift "to see ourselves as others see us." Poor Burns! this was as high as he could be expected to go. But how much more to be desired is it, that we could see ourselves as *God* sees us? Not indeed at once, lest the very sight should sink us, forthwith, into everlasting night; but by degrees, rather, as we may be able to endure it.

How much to be desired is it, I say, especially by the young, that we might see how prone we are to enter into competition, particular or general, with the community; and how apt we are, with almost every breath, and in almost every conceivable form, to throw the good character, and merits, and success, even, of others into the shade. How can those whose young hearts beat high in anticipation of a good name, even in this world, be willing to jeopardize their character by the commission of so much meanness!

I need not enter into particulars, especially when the invaluable work of Mrs. Opie is before the world. Let me refer those who entertain doubts whether, after all, I am not among the very sort of detractors whom I am censuring with so much severity—and whether, what I complain of in the individual, as abusive on here and there a neighbor or acquaintance, I am not pouring, by wholesale, and with a spirit not a whit better, upon a whole community,—let me refer all such, I say, to that invaluable work. Let me also refer them to themselves.

I am sure no one can carefully examine and analyze her own most secret feelings without discovering in herself the spirit of detraction in some form or other, if it be only in the form of genteel slander, envy or discontent. If there be those who do not find it so with themselves, and who say that however it may be with others, they are not thus circumstanced or thus guilty, I pity them most sincerely, as grossly ignorant of themselves. Such persons I have only and lastly to refer to that volume of Divine Truth, which assures us that the heart is deceitful above all things and desperately wicked; and which asks, with the most pertinent significance, not to say eloquence-WHO CAN KNOW IT?

CHAPTER XV.

THE RIGHT USE OF TIME.

Great value of moments. An old maxim. Wasting shreds of time. Time more valuable than money. What are the most useful charities. Doing good by proxy. Value of time for reflection. Doing nothing. Rendering an account of our time at the last tribunal.

On this subject—the right use of time—sermons, not to say volumes, without number, have been written; and yet it is still true, as an eminent poet has well said, that the individual "is yet unborn who duly weighs an hour."

But my business is not so much to dwell at large on the value of time in its larger divisions, such as days and hours, as to urge, in the first place, an attention to moments. "Take care of the pence," says an old but just maxim, "and the pounds will take care of themselves;" and it is somewhat so in regard to time. Take care of the moments, and the hours and days will take care of themselves.

Not, indeed, that hours and even days are not wasted, and worse than wasted; but the great error is, in disregarding the value and slighting the use of those smaller fragments of which hours, days and years are made. Show me the individual, young or old, who sets any thing like a just value on moments of time, and you will show me the person who values, in a proper manner, its larger divisions.

I have ventured upon this hackneyed subject, because I have often thought that young women—more, if possible, than most other young persons—need to be reminded of the unspeakable importance of moments. It is only a minute or two, many will say, or seem to say; and so they let time pass unemployed. But these leisure moments are frequently recurring; and the more they are slighted and wasted, the more they will be. And what is worse, she who frequently says, It is only a minute-and who makes this serve as an apology for wasting it—will soon extend the same apology to much larger portions of time. The current of human nature is ever downward: let those who love improvement and desire to be improved, remember it is so; and let them ever be mindful, in this respect, of their danger.

There are thousands who suffer themselves to waste shreds of time which might be applied to the attainment of knowledge—valuable knowledge—or to the work of doing good in a world where so much good needs to be done, who would not be willing to waste the smallest sum of money. I would not speak lightly of the habit of wasting money; but it must be admitted by all, that she who wastes, without remorse of conscience, her precious moments which might be usefully employed—if not in action, at least in conversation, or reading, or reflection—and yet would not, on any account, waste a cent of money, is justly chargeable, in a moral point of view, with straining out a gnat, and swallowing a camel.

For it should never be forgotten, that however valuable money may be, time is much more so. It is much more so, even as a means of doing good. There are very many persons, it is true, who seem to think otherwise. They seem not to think that they can do good with any thing but money.

Let us reflect, however, that no charity is more truly valuable, than visiting and aiding the sick, encouraging the depressed, instructing the ignorant, &c. Now is not she who does the latter, more sure of doing good than she who only gives the former? In the latter case, she bestows the very thing which is truly needful; in the former case, she only bestows that which is a means of doing good. These means may or may not be properly applied; of this the donor cannot be certain. But when, instead of giving money or doing good by proxy, she does it herself, the work is done, and done in her own way: and if not done well, she is responsible. She is not made, in that case, responsible for her neighbors.

But is *all* time wasted that is not spent in action, as some of my remarks might seem to imply? By no means. I have already spoken, in this chapter, of the use of time for reflection; and in a preceding one, have dwelt more especially on the value of solitude at certain seasons. What I mean to urge is, the folly of trifling away time in absolutely doing nothing. There is a sort of listlessness—or, perhaps, more properly, reverie—in which many indulge, which is as sinful as it is unprofitable; and there are modes of thinking and subjects of thought, which are, to say the least, unworthy of a rational, intelligent and immortal spirit.

I am not sure that there are not times—very short seasons, I mean—during our waking hours, even with those who are in tolerable health, when we best serve God and our fellow men by doing absolutely nothing at all. I am not sure, I say, that thus may not be the case. Still, if it is so, we should be exceedingly careful not to run into excess in this respect—an error which seems to be almost inevitable. For one who spends too little time in doing nothing, it is believed a thousand spend too much in this way. And let it never be forgotten, that not only for every idle word, but for every misspent moment, we are, according to Scripture, to render an account in the day when God will judge the secrets of each heart, according to the gospel of our Lord and Saviour Jesus Christ.

How valuable—how immensely valuable—will a few, only, of those moments which we now let slip with so much readiness, appear to us in that great day! What would we not then give for them? Five minutes here, spent in listlessness, or in doing absolutely nothing; five there, spent in idle or wicked conversation; and five there, in unnecessary attentions to our person or dress—how will the ghosts, as it were, of these departed seasons, haunt and torture us! Though willing to give worlds to recall them—not only for the sake of our own souls, but for those of others—thousands of worlds cannot buy them. No, not one solitary five minutes. Happy is she who "wastes not," that she may "want not," here or hereafter.

CHAPTER XVI.

LOVE OF DOMESTIC CONCERNS.

Reasons for loving domestic life. 1. Young women should have some avocation. Labor regarded as drudgery. 2. Domestic employment healthy. 3. It is pleasant. 4. It affords leisure for intellectual improvement. 5. It is favorable to social improvement. 6. It is the employment assigned them by Divine Providence, and is eminently conducive to moral improvement. The moral lessons of domestic life. A well ordered home a miniature of heaven.

I have incidentally made a few remarks on this subject elsewhere; but its importance demands a further and more attentive consideration.

There are numerous reasons which might be mentioned, why a young woman ought to cultivate a love of domestic life, and of domestic concerns; but I shall only advert to a few of them.

1. Every young woman should have some avocation, or calling. The Jews formerly had a proverb, that whoever of their sons was not bred to a trade, was bred to the gallows; and both Mohammedans and Pagans have maxims among them which amount to the same thing. But is that which is so destructive to the character of young men—I mean the want of proper employment—entirely harmless to young women? It surely cannot be.

True it is, and deeply to be regretted, that there is a fashionable feeling abroad, which is the reverse of all this. Both men and women, in fashionable life, are apt to regard all labor—not only manual, but mental—as mere drudgery. They will labor, perhaps, if they cannot help it; but seldom, if they can. Or at least, this seems to be their feeling when they begin a course of industrious action. Some, it is confessed, finally become so much accustomed to action, that they continue it, either as a matter of mere habit, or because its discontinuance would now render them as miserable as they were in breaking up their natural indolence, and in forming their present industrious habits.

2. She should love the concerns and cares of domestic life, because no ordinary employment contributes more, on the whole, to female health.

I do not mean to say, that there is no other kind of employment which *could* be rendered equally healthy with doing house-work; but only that, as a whole, and especially in the present state of public sentiment, this is decidedly the best. Perhaps, in some circumstances, moderate labor—labor proportioned to her strength-in the field, or in the garden, might be healthier, were she trained to it; but as things and customs now are, this can hardly be done.

3. The employment is a pleasant one. It has at once all the advantages of a shelter from the severe cold of the winter, and of seclusion from the sultry sun of summer, and the storms of winter and summer both. [Footnote: Perhaps it may be said, that woman actually suffers more from the extremes of heat and cold, than man, notwithstanding her seclusion, This may be true; but I still think her constitution is not quite as liable to *injury*, from the weather, as that of man; besides which, she is rather less liable to accidents.] And not only is the house-keeper favored in these respects, but in many others. A pleasant, well ordered home, is perhaps the most perfect representation of the felicity of the heaven above, which the earth affords. At any rate, it is a source of very great happiness; and woman, when she is what she should be, is thus made a conspicuous agent in communicating that happiness.

Are not, then, home, and the domestic concerns of home, desirable? Are they not agreeable? Or if not, should not every young woman strive to make them so? How then does it happen that an idea of meanness is attached to them? How does it happen that almost every young woman who can, gets rid of them—as almost every young man does of farming and other manual labor.

4. Home affords to young women the means and opportunities of intellectual improvement. I do not mean to affirm, that the progress they can make in mere science, amid domestic concerns, will be quite as great in a given time—say one year—as it might be in many of our best schools. But I do mean to say, that it might be rapid enough for every practical purpose. I might say, also, that young women who study a little every day under the eye of a judicious mother, and teach that little to their brothers and sisters, will be more truly wise at the end of their pupilage, than they who only study books in the usual old fashioned—I might say, rather, new fashioned—manner. It is in these circumstances more strikingly true than elsewhere, that

"Teaching, we give; and giving, we retain."

5. But once more. She who is employed in the domestic circle, is more favorably situated—I mean, if the domestic circle is what it should be—for social improvement, than she could be elsewhere. She may not, it is true, hold so much converse on the fashions—or be a means of inventing, or especially of retailing, so much petty scandal—as in some other situation, or in other circumstances. Still, the society of home will be better and more truly refined, than if it were more hollow, and affected, and insincere—in other words, made up of more fashionable materials. If to be fashionable is to distort nature as much as possible—and if the most fashionable society is that which is thus distorted in the highest degree—then it must be admitted that home cannot always be the best place for the education of young women.

6. But, lastly, young women should love domestic life, and the care and society of the young, because it is, without doubt, the intention of Divine Providence that they should do so; and because home, and the concerns of home, afford the best opportunities and means of moral improvement.

The prerogative of woman—the peculiar province which God in nature has assigned her—has been already alluded to with sufficient distinctness. Let every reader, then, follow out the hint, and ask herself whether it is not important that she should love the place and circumstances thus assigned her; and whether she who hates them, is likely to derive from them the great moral lessons they are eminently designed to inculcate.

Is it asked what moral lessons, so mightily important, can be learned in the nursery and in the kitchen? In return, I may ask, what lessons of instruction are there which may *not,* be learned there, and what moral virtues may not there be cultivated? Each family is a world in miniature; and all the necessary trials of the temper and of the character, are usually found within its circle.

Are we the slaves of appetite? Here is the place for learning the art of self-government. Are we fretful? Here we may learn patience: for a great fund of patience is often demanded; and the more so as we are apt, here, to be off our guard, and to yield to our unhappy feelings.

There are thousands who succeed very well in governing themselves—their temper and their passions— while the eye of the world is upon them, who, nevertheless, fail most culpably in this respect, when at home, secluded, as they seem to think themselves, from observation. Hence the importance of great effort to keep ourselves in subjection in these circumstances; and hence, too, the value of a well ordered and happy home.

Are we over-fond of excitement? Home is a sufficient cure for this—or may be made so to those who ardently desire that it should be. Are we desirous of forming our character upon the model of heaven? We are assured, from the Author of Holy Writ, that the kingdom of heaven consists in that simplicity, confidence, faith and love, which distinguish the child.

In short—to repeat the sentence—there is no place on earth so nearly resembling the heaven above, as a well ordered and happy family. If your lot is cast in such a family, young reader, be thankful for the favor, and strive to make the most of it. Not merely as a preparation for standing at the head of such a family yourself; not merely as a preparation for the work of teaching—although for this avocation I know of nothing better; not merely because it is your duty, and you feel that you *must* do it; but because it is for your happiness—yes, even for your life.

All character is formed in the school of trial; all good or valuable character, especially. And—I repeat the sentiment—in no place or department of this school are circumstances so favorable for such a purpose, as what may, emphatically, be termed the *home department.* The family and the church are God's own institutions. All else, is more or less of human origin: not, therefore, of necessity, useless—but more or less imperfect. She who would obey the will of God in forming herself according to the divine mode, must learn to value those institutions, in some measure, as they are valued by Him, and love them with a degree of the same love wherewith He loves them.

It will here be seen that I value domestic avocations so highly—giving them, as I do, the preference over all other female employments—not as an end, but as a means. It is because they secure, far better—other things being alike—the grand result at which every female should perpetually aim—the attainment of excellence. It is because they educate us far better, physically, socially and morally—and with proper pains and right management, they might do so intellectually—than any other employment, for the great future, towards which we are every day hastening.

This home school is—after all which has been said of schools and education—not only the first and best school, especially for females, but emphatically *the* school. It is the nursery from which are to be transplanted, by and by, the plants which are to fill, and beautify, and perfect—if any perfection in the matter is attained—all our gardens and fields, and render them the fields and gardens of the Lord. Ton much has not been—too much cannot be—said, it appears to me, in favor of this home department of female education—especially as a means of religious improvement.

Young women thus trained, would not only be most fitly prepared for the employment which, as a general rule, they are to follow for life, but for every other employment to which they can, in the good providence of God, ever be called. No matter what is to be their situation—no matter even if it is merely mechanical, as in some factory, or as an amanuensis—this apprenticeship in the family is not only highly useful, but, as it seems to me, indispensable. Is not mind, and health, and self-government—yes, and self-knowledge, too—as indispensable to the individual who is confined to a bench or desk, as to any person who is more active? Nay, are they not even much more so—since sedentary employments have, in themselves, as respects mind and character, a downward, and narrowing, and contracting tendency?

CHAPTER XVII.

FRUGALITY AND ECONOMY.

Economy becoming old fashioned. The Creator's example. Frugality and economy should be early inculcated. Spending two pence to save one, not always wrong. Examples of disregarding economy. Wasting small things. Good habits as well as bad ones, go by companies. This chapter particularly necessary to the young. Frugality and economy of our grand-mothers.

Economy is another old fashioned word, which, like the thing for which it stands, is fast going into disrepute; and in these days, it will require no little moral courage in him who has any thing of reputation at stake, to commend it—and above all, to commend it to young women. What have they to do with economy? thousands might be disposed to ask, were the subject urged upon their attention.

"Is there not something connected with the idea of economy, which tends, necessarily, to narrow the mind and contract the heart?" This question, too, is often asked, even by those whom age and experience should have taught better things.

I am pained to find the rising generation so prone to discard both frugality and economy, and to regard them as synonymous with narrowness, and meanness, and stinginess. There cannot possibly be a greater mistake.

May I not ask, without incurring the charge of irreverence, if there is any thing more obvious, in the works of the Creator, than his wonderful frugality and good economy? Where, in his domain, is any thing wasted? Where, indeed, is not every thing saved and appropriated to the best possible purpose? And will any one presume to regard his operations as narrow, or mean, or stingy?

What can be more abundant, for example, than air and water? Yet is there one particle too much of either of them? Is there one particle more than is just necessary to render the earth what it was designed to be? Such a thing may be said, I acknowledge, by the ignorant, and short-sighted, and incautious. They vent their occasional complaints, even against the Ruler of the skies, because the windows of heaven are, for a time, shut up, and the rain falls not; and yet these very persons are constrained to admit, in their more sober moments, that all is ordered about right.

Be this as it may, however, there can be no doubt that a just measure of frugality and economy is a cardinal virtue, and should be early inculcated, even though it cost us some time and effort.

A great deal has been said, and no small number of words wasted, in endeavoring to show the folly of spending two pence to save one; whereas, to do so, in some circumstances, may be our highest wisdom. If it be important to learn the art of *saving*—the art of being *frugal*—then the art should be acquired, even if it costs something in the acquisition. No one thinks of reaping the full reward of adult labor in any occupation, the moment he begins to put his hand to it, as a mere apprentice. Does he not thus, in learning his occupation or trade—especially during the first years—spend two pence to save one? Does not all preparation for the future, obviously involve the same necessity?

I do not, certainly undertake to say that it is always proper—or indeed, that it is often so—to spend more, in order to save less. I only contend that it is sometimes so; and that to do so, may not only be a matter of propriety, but also a duty.

Let me give an example. Young women are sometimes apt to acquire a habit of being wasteful in regard to small things, such as pins, needles, &c. Yet, to teach them, in these days of refinement, always to pick up pins when they see them lying before them on the floor or elsewhere, and put them into a pin-cushion, or in some suitable place, would no doubt be considered as quite unreasonable.

But would not such a habit be exceedingly useful? Am I to be told that it would be a great waste, since the value of the time consumed in thus picking up pins and needles, would be more than twice the value of the articles saved? Am I to be told that this is not only spending two pence to save one, but that it is actually wicked? If so, by what art shall a wasteful young woman be taught good habits?

I would certainly urge a young girl who was careless about pins, needles, &c., to form the habit of picking up every one she found. I would do so, to prevent her prodigal habits from extending to other matters, and affecting and injuring her whole character. But I would also do so, to cure the bad habit already existing. More than even this; I advise every young woman who finds herself addicted to habits which are opposed to a just frugality and economy, to begin the work of eradicating them, without waiting for the promptings of her mother and friends. Nor let her, for a moment, fear the imputation of meanness; it is sufficient for her that she is doing what she knows to be right.

Good habits, as well as bad ones, like virtues and vices, are apt to go in company. If one is allowed, others are apt to follow. First, those most nearly related; next, those more remotely so; and finally, perhaps, the whole company.

I would not dwell long on a subject like this, in a book for young women, were I not assured that the case requires it. I see young women every where, especially among the middling and higher classes, and in great numbers too, exceedingly improvident; and not a few of them, wasteful. The world seems to be regarded as a great store-house which can never be exhausted, let them be as extravagant as they may. They forget, entirely, the vulgar but correct adage, that "always taking out of the meal tub, and never putting in, soon comes to the bottom"-and seem to take it for granted there is no bottom to their resources.

Our grand-mothers—our great grand-mothers, rather—were not ashamed of frugality or economy. They were neither afraid nor unwilling to do what they knew to be right, simply because it happened to be unfashionable. I am not, indeed, either constitutionally or by age, one of those who place the golden age exclusively in the past. I can see errors in the conduct of our grand-mothers. But I also see in them excellencies; many virtues of the sterner, more sober sort, which have been bartered for modern customs—not to say vices—at a very great loss by the exchange. What we have thus lost, I should be glad, were it possible, to restore.

CHAPTER XVIII.

SYSTEM.

General neglect of system in families. Successful efforts of a few schools. Why the effects they produce a not permanent. Importance of right education. Here and there system may be found. Blessedness of having a mother who systematic. Let no person ever despair of reformation. How to begin the work.

There is hardly any thing which the majority of our young women hate—frugality and economy, and the study of themselves, perhaps, excepted—so much as *system*. In this respect a few of our best schools have, within a few years, attempted something; and, in a few instances, with success. I could mention several schools for females, whose teachers have done much more good by the habits of order and system they have inculcated and endeavored to form, than by the sciences they have taught.

The tendency of this excellent feature of a few of our institutions is, however, pretty effectually counteracted by the general feeling of the public, that the school is but a place of painful though necessary restraint; and that when it is over, study is over—and with it, all the system which had been either inculcated or practised. And though not a few who have been thus compelled to live by system, for two or three years, see plainly its excellent effects, and both they and their parents acknowledge them, still the school is no sooner terminated, than every thing of the kind is very likely to become as though it had never been.

So long, however, as home is home, and all the associations therewith are as delightful as they now are— and so long as the greater number of our families live at random, regarding order as constraint, and method and system as slavery—just so long will the feelings of the young of each rising generation, revolt at every thing like order and system; and though for the sake of peace, as well as other and various reasons, they may be willing to conform to both, for a time, yet will they sigh, internally, for the hour when their bondage shall cease, and the day of their emancipation arrive. It is not in human nature, to look back to the scenes, and customs, and methods—if methods they deserve to be called, where all is at random—of early life, without a fondness for, and an inward desire to return to them; and there are few so hardened as not to do it whenever an opportunity occurs. How important, then—how supremely so—is right education! How important to sow, in the earliest years, the seeds of a love of order and system! How important to young women, especially, that this work should not be deferred; since if it is so, it is most likely to be deferred forever.

I know, full well, that here and there a house-keeper, convinced in her conscience that she can do vastly more for herself and others, as well as do it better, by means of system, than without it, attempts something like innovation upon the usual random course which prevails about her. She resolves to have her hours of labor, her hours of recreation, and her hours of reading and visiting. She believes life is long enough for all the purposes of life. She is resolved to be systematic on Sabbath and on week days; in the common details of the family; in dress; and in regard to the hours of rising, meals and rest. But she has a herculean task to accomplish—no small part of which is, to bring her husband and the other members of her family to co-operate with her. Yet, amid every discouragement, she perseveres, and at length succeeds. Is not such a victory worth securing?

Let the young woman who has such a person as I have just described, for her mother, rejoice in it. She can never be too grateful, not only to her mother, but to God. Her life is likely to be of thrice the usual value.

Our daughters who are blessed with such mothers, may become as polished corner stones in a temple—worthy of themselves, of those who educate them, and of God.

But let not those who have been less fortunate, in respect to maternal training and influence, utterly despair. Convinced of the general correctness of the views here advanced, and desirous of entering on the work of reform, let them take courage, and begin it immediately. Though the mother, by her influence in the early formation of character, is almost omnipotent, she is not quite so. Though the Ethiopian cannot change his skin, nor the leopard his spots, still it is not utterly impossible for those to do well who have been long accustomed to do evil. "What has been done," you know, "*can* be done." Make this maxim your motto, and go forward in the work of self-education. But remember to begin, in the first place, with the smaller matters of life; and to conquer in one point or place of action, before you begin with another. And, lastly, remember not to rely wholly on your own strength. You are, indeed, to work—and to work with all your might; but it is always God that worketh in you, when any thing effectual is accomplished, in the way of improvement.

CHAPTER XIX.

PUNCTUALITY.

Evil of being one minute too late. Examples to illustrate the importance of punctuality. Case of a mother at Lowell. Her adventure. General habits which led to such a disaster. Condition of a family trained to despise punctuality.

No system can be carried on without both order and punctuality. I have already said something, incidentally, on both of these topics; but their importance entitles them to a separate consideration.

The importance of strict punctuality could be shown by appealing to hundreds of authorities; but I prefer an appeal to the good sense of my readers.

How painful it is, in a thousand instances of life, to be but one minute too late; and how much evil it may, indeed, often does occasion, both to ourselves and others!

"Think of the difference," says a spirited writer, "between arriving with a letter one minute before the post-office is closed, and arriving one minute after; between being at the stage-office a quarter of an hour too soon, and reaching there a quarter of an hour too late; between shaking a friend heartily by the hand as he steps on board his vessel bound to the Indies, and arriving at the pier when the vessel is under weigh, and stretching her wide canvass to the winds! Think of this, and a thousand such instances, and be determined, through life, to be in time."

Allow me to illustrate the important subject of which I am now treating, by the case of a young mother. She wishes to go from Boston to Lowell. She leaves Boston in the cars which go at eleven, and reach Lowell soon after twelve. She goes to spend the afternoon with a sick friend there, resolving to return at five—the hour when the last cars leave Lowell for Boston. Her infant is left, for the time, in the hands of a maiden sister—the husband being engaged in his shop, and hardly knowing of her departure.

She spends the afternoon with her friend, and her services are very acceptable. But ere she is aware, the bell at the railroad depot rings for passengers to Boston. A few moments are spent in getting ready and in exchanging the parting salutation with those friends who, though aware of the danger of her being left, have not the honest plainness to urge her to make speed. She is, at length, under way; but on arriving at the depot, lo! the cars have started, and are twenty or thirty rods distant.

What can she do? "Time and tide," and railroad cars, "wait for none." It is in vain that she waves her handkerchief; the swift-footed vehicles move on, and are soon out of sight! She returns, much distressed, to the house of her sick friend, unfit to render her any further service-to say nothing of the mischief she is likely to do by exciting her painful sympathies.

But how and when is she to get home? There are no public means of conveyance back to the city till to-morrow morning, and the expense of a private conveyance seems to her quite beyond her means.

How could I be so late? she says to herself. How could I run the risk of being thus left? Why was I not in season? What will my husband think—especially as I came off without saying any thing to him about coming? But this, though much to distress her, is not all, nor the most. Her poor bade! what will become of that? Her friends endeavor to soothe her by diverting her mind—but to no purpose, or nearly none: she is half distracted, and can do nothing but mourn over her folly in being so late.

But the weather is mild, and all is propitious without, except that it is likely to be rather dark; and by means of the efforts of thoughtful friends, a coach is fitted out with a careful driver, to carry her home this very evening. It will take five hours in all; and as it is now six, she will reach home at about eleven. The infant will not greatly suffer before that time.

Finding herself fairly on the road, her feelings are somewhat composed, and she just now begins to think what her husband will do, when he comes from the shop at seven, and finds she has not arrived. She is afraid he will be at the extra pains and expense to come after her; and perhaps in the darkness pass by her, and go on to Lowell.

And her fears are partly realized. After much anxiety and some complaining—which, however, I will not undertake to justify—the husband is on the road with a vehicle, going to Lowell to assist her in getting home. They meet about half way from place to place, and the drivers recognize each other—though rather more than, in the darkness, could have been expected. The coach from Lowell returns, and that from Boston, taking in both passengers, wheels them back in haste to their home. In their joy to find matters no worse, they forget to recriminate each other, and think only of the timid sister with whom the infant was left in charge: for in the hurry of getting off, the husband had made no provision for quieting her fears of being alone. She passes the time, however, in much less mental agitation than might have been expected, and takes as good care as she can, of a fretful, crying, half-starved babe. As the clock strikes one, the family are all quiet in bed, and endeavoring to sleep.

How much uneasiness is here caused by being just about one minute (and no more) too late! And whence came it? Not by her not knowing she was running a risk by being tardy. Not that she had no apprehensions of evil. Not because her conscience was uneducated, or unfaithful. It was neither, nor any of these. There was, in the first place, a little want of decision. She suffered herself to vacillate between a sense of duty and the inclination to say a few words more, or bestow another parting kiss. And in the second place, it was the wretched habit she had always indulged, of delaying and deferring every thing she put her head or her hand to, till the very last moment.

I will give you a brief but correct account of her general habits. Not that the picture is a very uncommon one, but that you may view it in connection with the anecdote I have related, and thus get a tolerable idea of the inconveniences to which the wretched habit of which I have spoken, is continually exposing her.

She makes it a rule—no, I will not say that, for she has no rules, but she has a sort of expectation on the subject—to rise at five o'clock. Yet I do not suppose she is up at five, six times in the year. She is never awake at that timer or but seldom, unless she is awakened. Her husband, indeed, makes it a sort of rule to wake her at that hour; but he, alas, poor man! has no roles for himself or others; and if he undertakes to awaken her at five, it is usually ten or fifteen minutes afterward; and if she is let alone, she is often in bed till half past five—oftener, indeed, than up earlier. The breakfast hour is six; but I never knew the family to sit down at six. It is ten minutes, fifteen minutes, thirty minutes, and sometimes forty-five minutes after six, before the breakfast is on the table. The fire will not burn, and the tea is not ready; or the milk or cream for the latter has not arrived; or something or other is the matter—so she says, and so she believes—and indeed sometimes so it is.

The dinner time is half past twelve-that is, professedly so; but it is not once in twenty times that they sit down much before one o'clock—and I have known it to be even later. So it is with supper; and I might add, with every thing else. If an engagement is made, directly or indirectly, positively or only implied, it is never fulfilled at the time. She is never in her seat at church, till almost every body else is in, and the services have commenced; although the kind, but too indulgent parson waits some five or ten minutes for his whole congregation—whom, alas! he has unwittingly trained to delay. In short, she does nothing, and performs nothing, punctually, not even going to bed; for this is deferred to a very late hour-sometimes till near midnight.

Now herein is the secret—the foundation, rather—of her trouble at Lowell. Had she been trained to punctuality in other things, she would, in all probability, have been punctual there. The misfortune which I have described, is but a specimen of what is ever and anon occurring in the history of her life.

Nor are her sufferings—though they are severe—from her unhappy habit, the end of the matter. I have already more than intimated that her companion has caught the disease; but it is still more visible in the conduct of her sons and daughters. They, like herself, seldom do any thing at the proper time. They are never punctual in their engagements, nor decided in their conduct. I know not, however, what the daughters may yet do—several of them being quite young. If they should chance to meet with better instructions than they are accustomed to receive—should take warning, and do all they can in the way of self-improvement—they may be able to break the chains of an inveterate and almost unconquerable habit, and make themselves useful in their day and generation.

I do think, most sincerely, that if all the rest of the world were disorderly, or fell short in matters of punctuality, the young woman should not do so. Let her, in every duty, learn to be in time. Let her resolve to do every thing a little before the time arrives; nothing, a moment after it.

The keeper of a boarding house, who is at the same time the principal of one of our most flourishing schools for both males and females, makes it a point to have every one of his boarders in their seats at dinner, when the clock strikes twelve, which is the appointed hour.

And the late principal of a very highly distinguished female school in Boston, used to have every exercise regulated by a clock kept in the room; and whatever else was going on—whether it was finished or unfinished—whenever the hour for another exercise arrived, it was attended to. The whole school, as if with one impulse, seemed to obey the hour, rather than the teacher. Such order and punctuality, every where and in every thing, constitute the beauty of life; and I was going to say, the beauty of heaven—of which this life should be a sort of emblem. Heaven, in any event, is not only a world of order, but of punctuality also; and she who goes there, must be prepared to observe both, or it will be no heaven to her.

As I have strongly insisted in respect to the formation of other important habits, so in regard to this. It must be commenced in the smaller matters of life. Let the young woman be in time—that is, be punctual—in the performance of what she regards as trifles, and when she becomes a matron, she will seldom be tardy in what are deemed the weightier matters.

I have spoken of the importance of punctuality, and have strongly insisted that whatever is worth doing at all, is worth doing well. I am now about to insist, with equal earnestness, that what is worth beginning and performing well, is worth doing thoroughly, or finishing.

Some young women never do any thing thoroughly—even the smallest matters. All their lives long, they live, as it were, by halves, and do things by halves. If they commence reading a book, unless it is something very enticing and exciting, they neither read it thoroughly nor finish it. Their dress is never put on thoroughly; and even their meals are not thoroughly eaten.

In regard to what is last mentioned, they fail in two respects. Either through fear that they shall be unfashionable, if they use their teeth, or from sheer carelessness in their habits, they never masticate their food thoroughly; and they never seem to get through eating. The true way is, to finish a meal in a reasonable time, and then let the matter rest; and never be found eating between meals. Whereas, the class of persons of whom I am speaking, seem never to begin or end a meal. They are nibbling, if food chance to fall in their way, all their lives long.

But—to return to other habits than those which pertain to eating and drinking—this want of thoroughness, of which I am speaking, wherever it exists in a young woman, will show itself in all or nearly all she does.

Suppose she is washing dishes, for example; something is left unwashed which ought to have been washed; something is left only partly washed; or the whole being done in a hurry, something is not set away in its place, and along comes a child and knocks it over and breaks it.

Perhaps site is sewing. She is anxious to get her work along; and though she know, how it ought to be done, she ventures to slight it especially if it is the property of another. Or having done it well till she comes near the end, the place where, perhaps, every thing ought to be particularly firm and secure—ought to be done thoroughly—she leaves a portion of it half done; and the garment gives way before it is half worn.

Or she is cooking; and though every thing else is well boiled, a single article is not well done—which gives an appearance of negligence to the whole. At any rate, it is not done well; and she gets the credit of not being a thorough house-keeper.

"For who hath despised the day of small things?" is a scriptural inquiry on a most important subject; and were it not likely to be construed into a want of reverence for sacred things, the same inquiry might be made in regard to the matter before us. There is a universal disposition abroad to despise small matters, and to stigmatize him who defends their importance.

One might suppose a young woman would find out the mischiefs that result from a want of thoroughness, by the inconvenience which inevitably results from it. It is not very convenient or comfortable, to be obliged to do a thing wholly over again, or suffer from want, because a piece of work, very trifling in itself, was not done thoroughly. Nor is it very convenient to go and wash one's hands every time a lamp is used, because it was not thoroughly cleaned or duly put in order, when it should have been. Nor is it easy to clean an elegant carpet which has become soiled, or replace a valuable astral lamp, or mirror, which has been broken, simply for the want of thorough attention in those who have the care of these things. These little inconveniences, constantly recurring, might rouse a person to reflection, one would think, as effectually as occasional larger ones. We do not, however, always find it so.

Young people ought to consider what a host of evils sometimes result from a slight neglect. The trite saying—"For want of a nail, the shoe was lost; for want of a shoe, the horse was lost; and for want of a horse, the rider was lost"—will, however, illustrate this part of my subject. Had the single nail which was omitted—the last one—been driven, and driven properly; had the work, in short, been done thoroughly, the shoe, horse and rider might all have been preserved.

Do not dread the imputation of being over-nice or whimsical, if you do your work thoroughly. You must learn to regard your own sense of right—your regard to duty—as a thing of far more importance than either the sneers or the approbation of thousands of the unthinking. I have heard an individual of great worth and respectability complain of a young friend of his, because he made it a point to finish thoroughly every thing he undertook, and charge him with having what he called a *mania* for finishing, I remember, too, a very worthy, and, in the main, excellent farmer, who used to complain of a very conscientious son of his, because, forsooth, he was determined to finish every thing he began, in the best possible manner, without paying much regard to the opinions of others. But these facts only show that wise and good men may not fully understand the nature and power of habit—or the necessity of being thorough in small as well as larger matters. The first individual I have named, was forever suffering from his own want of thoroughness—and was miserable through life; and the last would have been far happier all his life time, had he been as much disposed to finish the things he undertook, as his son.

CHAPTER XX.

EXERCISE.

The muscles, or moving power of the body. Their number and character. Philosophy and necessity of exercise. Why young women should study these. Various kinds of exercise. 1. Walking. 2. Gardening and agriculture. 3. House-keeping. 4. Riding. 5. Local exercises.—Difficulty of drawing the public attention to this subject. The slavery of fashion. Consequences of the of fashionable neglect of exercise. A common but shocking sight.

This is a highly important subject; and it is connected with an unusual variety of topics. I beg the reader to exercise a little patience, therefore, if, on this account, I extend it to an unusual length.

It should not be forgotten, that the human body is moved from place to place, at the direction of the will, through the intervention of what are called muscles—of which there are in connection with the whole human frame, from four hundred to five hundred.

They are long bundles or portions of lean flesh, usually a little flattened and somewhat rounded at their edges, and terminating at one end—often at both—in a harder, flatter, white substance, called tendon, which is fastened to the bone.

But I need not—and indeed I cannot—in a work like this, enter upon a minute account of the human frame, or of any considerable portion of it; especially so considerable a portion of it as the bony and muscular systems. For such information, I must refer the reader to the work alluded to in a previous chapter—"The House I Live In"—and, if her leisure time will justify it, to still more extended works on anatomy and physiology, which can be easily obtained.

Of the philosophy, and even the necessity, of exercise, however, I need only say, in the present place—in addition to what has been said already—that much of human health and happiness depends on the proper development, and cultivation, and daily exercise of the whole muscular system; and that the health, and happiness, and usefulness of young women, are not less dependent on the right condition of the physical frame—the bones and muscles among the rest—than in the case of other classes of persons. I might even say, that of all classes of people in the world—parents and teachers alone excepted—young women are most imperiously called upon to attend to this subject.

It will now be my object to speak of the various kinds of exercise for young women; and to treat of them in what I conceive to be the order of their value.

1. *Walking.*—If I were residing in Great Britain, and writing for the perusal of young women there, I suppose it would hardly be necessary to urge very strongly the importance of walking as an exercise; for we are told by accredited travellers, that not only females of the middle and lower classes, but those of rank, also, are accustomed to this form of exercise, to an extent which would surprise the young women of this country. Neither do they go out attired in such a manner that a single drop of water would annoy them, or spoil their happiness; but they go prepared for the task. They have, as I understand, their coarser clothes, and shoes, and head-dresses, for the purpose.

But here, in the United States—among the female sex, especially—walking, like house-keeping and agriculture, has been, of late years, regarded as drudgery—fit for none but the poor, or the mean, or the eccentric. And when performed, it is seldom done in the love of it.

Now it is well known to those who have studied the subject of exercise, that, though walking is of inestimable importance—second, in all probability, to no other form of mere exercise—it is, nevertheless, of far the most value, when it is undertaken and pursued with pleasure. While, therefore, I recommend it to young women, I do it in the hope that they will not regard it as task-work—as mere drudgery. I hope they will regard it as a source of pleasure and happiness.

To render it such, something more is required than merely to walk, in a solitary manner, to a certain stone, or tree, or corner, or house—the mind all the while unoccupied by any thing agreeable or useful—and then to return as listless as they came. Such exercise, it is true, will move the limbs, and do much to keep the bones and muscles in a healthy state; and by the gentle agitation which is induced, will promote the circulation of all the fluids, and the due performance of all the functions of the body—except the function which pertains to the brain and nervous system. It will do all this, I say; but it will not do it so well, if the exercise is performed as a piece of task-work, as it would if it were done cheerfully and voluntarily.

I counsel the young woman, therefore, who wishes to derive the utmost possible benefit from walking, to contrive to make the exercise as agreeable as possible. To this end, she should endeavor to have before her—I mean before her mind—an agreeable object; or at least she should be accompanied by an agreeable companion. Both are desirable; but one of the two is indispensable.

As to the kind of object which should be held in view, I cannot, of course, say much; nor need I—for it makes but little difference, so far as the physical benefit to be derived from it is concerned. In regard to the moral and intellectual advantages, however, which are to be derived from it—to herself and to others—it makes a very great difference indeed. She who goes in company with one or two, or a small number of companions, on some benevolent errand—some work of mercy to the ignorant, the sick, or the distressed—at once secures all the physical, the intellectual, and the moral advantages to be derived by herself, and confers inestimable blessings on others.

Let it not be said that it is not he duty of young women to go on such errands of mercy. I know of no neighborhood, containing the small number of twenty families, in which there are not individuals who need to be fed, clothed, enlightened, encouraged, warmed or elevated. The more elevated their present condition, as a general rule, the more can be done to raise them still higher. The destruction of the poor, is their poverty; and in like manner, the destruction of the ignorant, is their ignorance. People must know something, in order to know more; and in like manner, must they possess something, in order to value our charities, and make a wise use of them.

If it should be urged, that in speaking of the advantages of walking, I have hitherto addressed myself to a small class of the community, only—that those who are compelled to labor, have not the time necessary for walks of love, instruction or charity—I reply, that this does not lessen the importance of what has been said to those individuals to whom it is applicable. Walking is nature's own exercise; and will always be her best, when it can be performed. Nor would many in New England think themselves so poor as to be unable to afford it, were they aware of a tenth part of its general importance, and did they but know how to live orderly and systematically. Two hours of active walking a day, are worth a great deal; and no one who can walk briskly and cheerfully, and without very great fatigue, *three* hours, need to complain of want of exercise. I must omit, of course, in a work like this, intended for young women, the mention of any motion more rapid than walking. Running, to those who have passed into their teens, would be unfashionable; and who could endure the charge of disregarding the fashions? Who could risk the danger of being regarded as a romp?

I am informed by a traveller of the most undoubted veracity, that females of the highest classes, in some parts of Europe—the daughters of Fellenberg, the Swiss educator, for example—do not hesitate, at times, to engage in the athletic and healthy exercises of skating and coasting. I have even been told that the same remark might be applied, to some extent, to the females of the state of Maine.

2. *Gardening and Agriculture.*—Here again I shall be treading on dangerous ground, as I am fully aware. As in the former ease, however, so in the present, I shall not be wholly alone. There are those who have dared to jeopardize their reputation by insisting on light agricultural and horticultural employments for females, young and old, who cannot, or who suppose they cannot find time for walking; and to the list of this sort of unfashionables, my name, I suppose, must be added. To those who do not and cannot enjoy the benefit of active and pleasurable walking abroad, these employments are unquestionably the best substitutes. When these are wholly depended upon for exercise, however, they should be pursued at least from two to four hours in a day; and the constitutions of some will require much more than even four hours.

Let not the hardy, healthy young woman alone, be employed in this manner. It is useful and necessary, indeed, to her; but it is still more so to her in whom, to a light skin with light eyes and hair, are joined a slender frame, a narrow chest, and an unnatural and sickly delicacy. Whether this delicacy is the result of staying in the house, almost entirely secluded from light, air, and the extremes of heat and cold, or is inherited, makes very little difference. She who has it needs a great deal of exercise.

3. *House-keeping.*—Next to walking, and agricultural and horticultural exercise, house-keeping—or, as it is familiarly called, house-work—is probably the most healthy, and ought to be the most agreeable. And yet the bare statement of the fact, will be enough to induce many a fair reader, as I doubt not, to turn aside with pain and disgust.

The reasons why this employment is so healthy, are many and various. One is found in the fact, that it requires such a variety of exercise. Like farming and gardening, it calls into action, in the course of a day, and especially in the course of a week, nearly every considerable muscle of the body.

All these exercises seem, at first view, to have some advantages over walking. It should be remembered however, that nearly every muscle, and tendon, and bone in the whole human frame, is agitated, if it is not employed, in walking; and if the limbs are employed much the most, still the continued action of the whole body, though gentle, is in a few hours quite sufficient for all the purposes of health.

Every young woman should be determined to attend to, and understand, every kind of house-work. If a few kinds—as washing, for example—seem to be beyond her strength, she should only attend to them in part, according as she is able. It is pitiable to see a young woman of twenty, twenty-five or thirty, who cannot make bread, or iron a shirt, or boil a pudding—ay, and who cannot make and mend clothes, if necessary—simply because she has never been required to do it. Still more pitiable is it, as I have already said, to find those who have never done it, because they thought it would be demeaning themselves—or because they have acted upon the principle of doing nothing for themselves or others, as long as they can help it.

It is scarcely possible that a young woman twenty years of age, has not had ample opportunities for learning to do all kinds of house-work, provided it has been her fixed resolution to improve them; and I am fully assured that house-keeping, actively and cheerfully pursued, in all its parts, is sufficient to secure a tolerable measure of health to every individual. And yet I am equally confident, that if walking, or out-of-door labor, were superadded to this, in the way I have proposed and recommended, she would derive from it many important advantages, besides being still healthier. Indeed, no person, in any employment whatever, is so healthy as to exclude all possibility of further improvement. It is not yet known how healthy an individual may become.

4. *Riding.*—Horseback exercise, for those who cannot enjoy any of the three modes of which I have already spoken, is excellent. It is particularly valuable where there is a tendency to lung complaints, whether induced by wearing too tight a dress, or in any other manner. It should not be forgotten, however, that if the chest is very greatly diseased, this exercise may be one of the worst which could be taken.

As to riding in a carriage, unless it is an open one, I must honestly say I do not like it, as an exercise for those who can secure that which is better. Indeed, except for a medicinal purpose, I always prefer one of the three kinds named above. And as for medicine, I would have young women so live, and especially so exercise, as to have no occasion for it. But on this subject I intend to say something in another place.

I do not believe life is long enough, in general, to allow us to indulge, to any great extent, either in what are commonly regarded as passive exercises, or in amusements, *as such:* I speak now of those who are above twelve years of age. Not that those who are over twelve, do not need amusement. I would have every thing amusing—or at least interesting. I mean simply to say, that walking, and running, and gardening, and farming, and house-keeping, usually involve enough of physical exercise for health; and that where these are duly attended to—or even any one of them—what are commonly called amusement's will hardly be needed. In earlier life, they unquestionably may be. But I do not think well of passive exercises for any person, so long as they can be avoided. And heterodox as the advice may be regarded, I cannot help counselling the young, above all, never to ride in an easy carriage, or a railroad, or in a steamboat or other vessel or ship, as long as they can pursue the lawful purposes of life, in a lawful and proper manner, by means of walking. It is soon enough to ride when we cannot walk.

Those who are desirous to glorify God in *whatever they do*, as Paul expresses it, will understand and feel the force of what I am now going to say; while those who make it their business, in this world, to seek happiness, without being careful to do it through the medium of personal excellence or holiness, will perhaps only smile at what they suppose is a mere eccentricity of opinion.

5. *Local Exercise.*—I have intimated that the bones and muscles, the brain and nerves, the stomach and intestines, the liver, the chyle apparatus, the lungs, and the skin; are all more or less exercised and benefited by walking, running, gardening, house-keeping, or riding on horseback. Still, other exercises will be necessary, in addition to all these. But much that I wish to say on these points will be found in subsequent chapters. It is only necessary for me to observe, in this place, that all the organs of the body, internal or external, together with all the senses, require, nay, demand, their appropriate or, as I might say, their particular exercise; and this, not only daily, but some of them much oftener.

The brain and nervous system require observation and reflection; and even, in my view, considerable hard study. This is their appropriate and necessary exercise. There are, indeed, those who exercise their brains too much; but for one who suffers from thinking too much, a dozen suffer from thinking too little.

The stomach and intestines require such food as will call them into proper action. That which is highly difficult of digestion may cause them to over-act; and this, to those whose vital powers are feeble, would be injurious. On the other hand, that which is too easy of digestion, will not afford the stomach exercise enough; and hence, in time, if its use is long continued, will be equally injurious. But once more. Concentrated substances—substances, I mean, consisting of pure nutriment, or that which is nearly so— such as oil, sugar, gum, &c.—do not afford the right kind of exercise to the stomach; for it is the appropriate work of this organ, and of the other internal organs—and not of machinery of human invention—to separate the nutritious part from that which is innutritious; and, therefore, that food affords the best sort of labor to the stomach which contains, along with a full supply of nutriment, a good deal of innutritious substance.

The exercise of the lungs consists not only in their full and free expansion in breathing, but in speaking, singing, &c., and even in laughing. Physiologists also consider sneezing, coughing and crying, especially the latter, as having their advantages, in early infancy, and perhaps, in same circumstances, even afterward.

In like manner do the eye and the ear, the tongue and the teeth, the hands and the face—and indeed every part of the system—require their appropriate exercise. This is not true of the merest infancy and childhood alone, but also, for the most part, of youth and manhood. Conversation, to a certain extent, is, for aught I know, as necessary to the health of the vocal organs, as to that of the lungs. Nor are the benefits of mastication confined wholly to the process of digestion. It is fully believed by distinguished physiologists, that the teeth themselves will last longer for being considerably used; and they seem to be borne out in this conclusion by facts. But if this is the case, what are we to think of the importance of light to the eye, sound to the ear, employment to the hands, &c.?

It is extremely difficult to induce the young to pay any attention to this important subject, as a matter of duty, even in some of its most obvious points and parts. Some of them will, it is true, use exercise enough of a particular kind, and at particular times; but the idea of attending to it as a matter of duty, is exceedingly hard for them to receive or entertain.

Few things are more pitiable, than the sight of young persons of either sex, so entirely enslaved to fashion, that they dare not labor in the garden, or the kitchen, or even walk briskly, lest somebody should observe and speak of it. It is not to be wondered at—trained as the young of both sexes are, to demand incessant excitement—that they should dislike walking, and every thing else of the more active kind, and sigh for the chaise, the coach, the sleigh, the car and the steamboat; but it does seem to me strange, that contrary to nature, they should seek their happiness in passive exercises alone, forgetful of their limbs, and hands, and feet. It is passing strange, that any tyrant should be able—even Fashion herself—so to change the whole current of human feeling, as to make a sprightly buoyant young girl of ten years of age, become at thirteen a grave, staid or mincing young woman, unable—rather, unwilling—to move except in a certain style, and then only with an effort scarcely exceeded by the efforts of those who are suffering from inquisitorial tortures.

No young woman who has a conscientious desire for improvement, and who is acquainted with the merest elements of physiological knowledge, could or would submit, for one day, to such abominable tyranny. She could not but be afraid thus to disobey the natural and reasonable laws of her Maker.

The consequences of this premature inactivity of the human frame, on the future well being of that frame, have never been half told: nor do I know that they can be—at least for some time to come.

I scarcely ever prescribed for one of these *staid* young women, without very great pain. To see a machine evidently made by its Almighty Architect for a great deal of motion, and made to run on with exactness for a hundred years or more, (were due care taken to preserve it in good order,) completely deranged, because Fashion says that motion is ungraceful or unbecoming—what, in a physical point of view, can be more lamentable!

To see woman denied, daily, by Fashion's nonsensical decrees, the pleasure which every healthy person feels in the use of his limbs, with their hundreds of muscles and tendons, and kept not only inactive, but almost secluded from air and light—who is not almost ashamed that he belongs to the same species? Yet such things are quite common among as, and they are constantly becoming more so.

CHAPTER XXI.

REST AND SLEEP.

Why rest and sleep are needed. Sleep a condition. We should sleep in the night. Moral tendency of not doing so. Is there any moral character in such things? Of rest without sleep. Good habits in regard to sleep. Apartments for sleep. Air. Bed. Covering. Temperature. Night clothing. Advice of Macnish on the number of persons to a bed. Preparation for sleep. Suppers. The more we indulge in sleep, the more sleep we seem to require. The reader indulged to study laws of rest and sleep. An appeal.

The moving powers of the human body are so constructed by the grand Mover of all things, that they require rest as well as action. And of the many hundreds of muscles and tendons in the living system, it is not known that there is one which could continue its action, uninterruptedly, for any considerable time, without serious injury. Even the muscular fibres of the heart rest a part of the time, between the beats and pulsations. Whether the brain—which is of course without muscular fibres—can act incessantly in the production of thought, is a question which I believe is not yet settled by meta-physicians. One thing we do know, however, which is, that if the other organs suffer for want of rest, we soon find that by the law of sympathy and otherwise, the brain and nervous system suffer along with them; and if our wakefulness is greatly protracted, they sometimes suffer very severely.

I have said that all the moving powers of the body require rest. They do; and in the young, a good deal of it. It is in vain for mankind—the young especially—to abridge their hours of sleep, whether for selfish or benevolent purposes. Sleep is made by the Creator a condition of our being and happiness; and he who complies not with this condition, is unworthy of the boon.

Sleep, moreover, should be had at the right season. It is useless to think of sleeping during the day-time, and keeping awake during the night, with impunity. For many facts are on record, showing in vivid colors the mischiefs which result, sooner or later, from thus turning day into night, and night into day. Need I present these facts? They are found, in greater or less numbers, in almost every work on health or physiology. I will present but one. It is from Valangin.

Two colonels in the French army, sometime ago, had a dispute whether it was most safe to march in the heat of the day, or in the evening. To ascertain this point, they obtained permission of the commanding officer to put their respective plans into execution. Accordingly, the one with his division marched during the day, although it was in the heat of summer, and rested all night. The other, with his men, slept in the day-time, and marched during the evening and part of the night. The result was, that the first performed a journey of six hundred miles without losing a single man or horse; while the latter lost most of his horses, and several of his men.

Of course, the inference from this, and other similar facts, is, that night is the time for sleep, and not day. Is it said that every person knows this? But every person does not practise accordingly. There are those who either do *not* know the fact—and not a few young women, too; may be found among the number—or who, knowing it, do not act according to their knowledge. Is it not more charitable to conclude they do not know the fact?

Franklin, indeed, once undertook to show, in his humorous way, that the inhabitants of Paris did not know that the sun gave light at its first rising. Whether they did know it or not—or whether or not they were culpable for their ignorance, provided it was voluntary—shall hold my readers to be as truly guilty of doing *that* wrong which is the result of their own voluntary ignorance, as if their minds were really enlightened. The young woman who goes to bed so late that she cannot wake till it has been day for some time—or who darkens her room on purpose that the day-light may not interrupt her repose when it comes—and who knows, at the same time, that it is wrong to sleep by day-light, except from the most absolute necessity—is as truly guilty, as if she slept by day-light with her windows open.

I believe the night is long enough for sleep in any latitude not higher than fifty degrees; and comparatively few of the human family reside much farther than this towards the poles.

The young woman who finds herself inclined to sleep after day-light, should resolve to break the habit as soon as possible. In order to do this, however, she should believe herself able to do it.

Here it will be rational to ask whether, after all, there is any moral character in the error, if it be one, of sitting up an hour later than usual, and then making it up by sleeping an hour after the arrival of day-light;—whether it is not a matter of *propriety*, merely, rather than a question of positive right or wrong in the sight of Heaven.

This question I have answered in the chapter on Conscientiousness—to which, in order to prevent repetition, I might refer the reader. If there be a sort of actions to which no character, good or bad, can justly be attached, then what did the apostle mean in requiring that *whatever we do* should be done to the glory of God? and where is the line to be drawn between those actions which are too small or too trifling to be worthy of having any right or wrong attached to them, and those which are not? But if every thing we do is either right or wrong, then there is a right and a wrong in regard to the particular class of actions of which I am just now treating.

The object of sleep should be to restore us, and fit us for renewed action. We may rest, to some extent, without sleep; as when we throw ourselves upon a sofa, or sit in an easy chair. Indeed, there is no hour of the day in which some portions of the moving powers are not resting, more or less. Still we cannot be wholly restored, in body and mind, without the soothing influence of

"Tired nature's sweet restorer, balmy sleep."

Every young woman should regulate her habits in regard to sleep and rest—not less than all her other habits—in such a way as will tend most to the good of her whole nature and as will consequently tend most to the glory of God. In other words, every person should be governed, in this matter, by true philosophy and Christian principle. This would lead to the following axioms or conclusions, every one of which is sustained by high authority.

Apartments for sleep should, if possible, be large and airy—and not on a ground floor, or in too dark a corner of the building.

The air of the room should circulate freely; although it is not considered safe to be exposed to currents of air. To this end, the bed should be rather large and loose; and should stand out from the all, and from the corners of the room; and should be without curtains, even in the coldest weather.

The bed ought to be rather hard; but it should, at any rate, be cool. Soft, yielding feather beds, in which the body sinks deeply, are very injurious, on account of the unnatural heat and perspiration they are sure to induce. It is of little consequence what the material of your bed is, if it be light, dry and porous, and not too soft. Straw, grass, husks, hair, and a great variety of other things, have been employed. Almost any thing—I repeat it—is better than feathers. The same remarks will apply to pillows.

We should sleep with as little covering as we can, and not actually feel cold and chilly. Most persons sleep under a great deal too much clothing. We require more in cold than in warm weather. We also require more on first going to bed, than when we get fairly warm but as it usually happens that we get warm and go to sleep at nearly the same time, it follows, that the clothing which was only sufficient to warm us, remains on the bed all night. We ought not to put on so much clothing as we are apt to do when we first go to bed—and then we shall not be likely to sleep all night under too much clothing, and wake up in the morning weakened by it.

The temperature of the room must never be overlooked. It should be as cold as it can well be made, and not be absolutely uncomfortable.

One reason for this is, that the oxygen, or vital principle of the air, which is more abundant in a given volume of cool air than in an equal amount of that which is warmer, will last longer when the room is cool, and the room will thus remain free from impurity.

Another reason is, that ratified air not only contains less oxygen in a given volume, as I have already said, but also appears to admit more readily of the admixture and thorough diffusion of bad gases. The carbonic acid gas which is formed by breathing, settles the more readily towards the floor, in proportion to the general density of the atmosphere of the room; and if the bed-room be large, so that it does not accumulate in such a quantity as to rise higher than the bedstead, it is less likely to be breathed over again, than if the atmosphere were more rare.

But there is still another reason for having our bed-clothes cool—though it is substantially the same with that mentioned in a preceding paragraph for having light rooms, beds, and light covering. We are greatly debilitated by sleeping unnecessarily warm. Our vital powers should be trained to generate a good deal of heat; and what they have been trained to do, they should continue to perform. All the heat, I say, therefore, which the body will manufacture for itself, readily, it should be permitted to do. But the moment we depend, unnecessarily, on external means of warmth—as too much or too soft and warm bed clothing, and too warm an atmosphere—that moment our internal organs begin to be enervated, in a greater or less degree, whether we are sensible of it or not.

We should not sleep in the clothes we have worn during the day. This is not on account of the heat it may induce, but on account of the bad air which our clothing confines. By having extra clothes for the night, and those very few indeed, and taking a little pains with those we have worn during the day—to hang them up and air them properly—we may do much towards keeping the pores of our bodies open, and preserving the skin in a clean state, and in a condition to perform its accustomed work.

We should also avoid damp clothing about our beds or bed-rooms. A healthy person may get slightly wet in the early part of the day, and even remain wet for a short time, especially if he continues in action, without injury: but it is by no means safe to sit down, or lie down, in wet or damp clothing; and it is more unsafe to do so at the close of the day, than it is in the morning. A vast amount of disease—colds, rheumatism, fever and consumption—is generated or aggravated in this way.

What I have here said of the conditions of sleep, is sustained, as I have already informed the reader, by high authority; I mean that of Macnish. He says, further, that "the practice of having two or three beds in one room, and two or three individuals in each bed, must be deleterious;" and that wherever it is necessary for more than one person to sleep in a single bed, "they should take care to place themselves in such a position as not to breathe in each others' faces." He also alludes to the custom of covering the head with the bedclothes—and calls it, as he ought to do, "a dangerous custom."

Macnish also gives the following directions on this subject:

"Before going to bed, the body should be brought into that state, which gives us the surest chance of dropping speedily asleep. If too hot, its temperature ought to be reduced by cooling drinks, [Footnote: By cooling drinks. Macnish cannot surely mean drinks of a low temperature, for these would be somewhat injurious in the evening. He means by cooling, not *heating* or *irritating*.] exposure to the open air, sponging, or even the cold bath. If too cold, it must be brought into a comfortable state by warmth. For both cold and heat act as stimuli, and their removal is necessary before sleep can ensue.

"A full stomach, also, though it sometimes promotes, generally prevents sleep; consequently, supper ought to be dispensed with, except by those who, having been long used to this meal, cannot do without it. As a general rule, the person who eats nothing for two or three hours before going to rest, will sleep better than he who eats a late supper. His sleep will also be more refreshing; and his sensations upon awaking, much more gratifying."

The cold bath at going to bed, taken to reduce our heat, because we are too warm, is of rather doubtful utility. Some may use it with entire safety; but to the feeble, or those who have been greatly over-heated or over-fatigued, it would be hazardous.

By supper, Macnish means, no doubt, that fourth meal so common in fashionable life, and not the usual third meal at six o'clock Those who never heard of a fourth, have no occasion for caution on this subject, except it be in regard to quantity. This third meal, however, even when it is eaten three hours before going to bed, should be light.

In order to sleep properly, let all the conditions which I have mentioned be faithfully observed. Then to these let there be added a most strict and conscientious regard for the rule which I have suggested in the beginning of this chapter—which is, to rise early. Let no young woman be found in bed after day-light, in the longest days; nor in the winter, after four o'clock.

Some will say, that at this rate they should not get sleep enough during the night; and should, as a consequence, either be dull during their waking hours, or be obliged to take a nap in the day-time. But if our hard-laboring people who rise at four o'clock in the summer, find time enough to sleep—most of them—without a nap in the day-time, surely they whose labor is not so hard, can do it. They cannot, I well know, if they sit up till ten or eleven o'clock at night.

If any one desires to glorify God in every thing she does, let her attend to the conditions I have mentioned. If she finds that in rising at daylight she does not get sleep enough, let her go to bed a little earlier. We ought to sleep about as much before midnight as after; and she who goes to bed at eight, and rises at four, will be pretty sure to get sleep enough. Few if any persons over twelve years of age, need more than eight hours sleep; and the greater proportion not so much.

Here I will mention one thing which does not seem to be generally known. The more we sleep, if we increase our sleep by degrees, the more we may. How far the time for sleep may be thus extended, I do not know. There are, indeed, circumstances which may make the same individual require less or more sleep, independent of the habit of indulgence: still it is true, as a general fact, that we may sleep as much or as little as we please.

When we increase the hours of sleep, however, it does not follow that we actually *sleep* more in the same proportion. Let an active individual, who has been accustomed to six hours, suddenly confine herself to four. Will her actual sleep be abridged one third? By no means. Nature will endeavor to make up for the loss of time by inducing sounder sleep.

In this, however, she is only in part successful. For those who sleep so very soundly, often sleep *too* sound. We are sometimes conscious, when we awake from an over-sound sleep, that we are not well refreshed; but whether conscious of it or not, it is so. Macnish says—"That sleep from which we are easily roused, is the healthiest; very profound slumber partakes of the nature of apoplexy."

A person who, having been in the habit of sleeping six hours in twenty-four, suddenly reduces the number to four, will, probably, for a time, sleep as much in four hours as she slept before in about five, or five and a half. But the *quality* of these five or five and a half hours' sleep will be inferior, and continue so, unless she arouses herself to an increased activity of her intellectual powers, and reduces the quantity of her food and drink.

I have supposed it to be generally known, that we need the more sleep, or seem to need it, in proportion as our minds are less active, and our bodily appetites hold us more in subjection. The individual, male or female, who approaches most nearly to the more stupid lower animals in point of intelligence, activity and general habits, will actually seem to require the most sleep; and, on the contrary, in proportion as an individual rises above all this, and becomes exceedingly active in mind, body and spirit, will the necessity for sleep be greatly diminished. Some of the most elevated of the human race, in point of intelligence, benevolence, and benevolent activity or spirituality have required but very little sleep. Of this number were Wesley, Matthew Hale, Alfred the Great, Jeremy Taylor, Baxter, Bishops Jewel and Burnet, Dr. John Hunter, Dr. Priestly, and Sobieski—as well as Frederick the Great, Gen. Elliot, Lord Wellington, and Napoleon. Of the same number, too, are some of our modern missionaries—to say nothing of several distinguished statesmen, among whom is Lord Brougham.

In view of these considerations, is there one of my readers, who, while she endeavors to sleep enough to answer every valuable purpose of her existence, on penalty of more or less suffering, will not guard, with the same assiduity, against sleeping too much? Aware that the more she indulges herself, the more she may, because she will become by so much the more stupid—and that the more she denies herself sleep, provided it is not to such an extent that her sleep becomes apoplectic, the more will her intellectual powers be developed and acquire the ascendency, and her animal nature be brought into subjection—will she not exert herself to the utmost, and pray for aid from on high, in striving to gain the victory over herself—her lower self—her animal self—and thus increase the duration and value of her existence?

I do not urge the consideration of the great amount of time, merely, which may be saved by rising early. Some have attempted to show that they who rise two hours earlier every morning than usual, gain an amount of time in sixty years—viz., from the age of ten to that of seventy—equal to about seven years of active life. Is it not obvious that there may be mistake here? For if she who rises two hours earlier, goes to bed as much earlier at right, no time is saved at all. And if without going to bed any earlier, she is rendered so much more dull or sleepy during the day, that she loses two hours, or even one, this will form a proportional deduction from her supposed gain. It is she only, who, while she sleeps all which her nature really demands, and takes care not to exceed the demand, succeeds also in lessening the demand itself, that is the real gainer.

It is a pitiable sight to see an immortal being, made in the image of Almighty God, and capable, by divine aid, of enjoying Him forever, rendering himself sleepy, brutish, or besotted, by the form of indulgence of which I am now speaking. And it seems to me still more pitiable—indeed, absolutely disgusting—to see females doing this; and especially, intelligent *young* women!

I wish every reader would take this subject of wasting time in sleep into serious, and conscientious, and prayerful consideration. Let her remember that her time is not hers, any more than she herself is her own; that both are "bought with a price"—an amazing price, too! How can she, then, waste time-a single moment of it? Yet people will do it. Hundreds, and thousands, and millions, will do it. Some will do it—many, I fear—who have professed the Christian name, and who believe that they bear in their bodies the marks of their dying Lord and Master.

I will close this chapter by briefly summing up what has been said. Let your sleep be in the night; not in the day-time. Let it be, moreover, in the *middle* of the night, as much as possible. To sit up till near midnight, and to get up just after midnight, are perhaps equally injurious, though not by any means equally common. Spend the close of each day at home; and go to bed early, with an empty or nearly an empty stomach, a cheerful temper, a quiet mind, and a good conscience. Let the air be pure, yourself pure, your clothing and bed simple and cool, and your room also cool. Wake with the first rays of the morning in summer, and about the same hour in winter. Get up as soon as you awake; and if your sleep has been insufficient, go to rest a little earlier the succeeding evening. Thus will you at once discharge your duty, and obtain peace here and hereafter.

CHAPTER XXII

INDUSTRY.

Education to industry. Man naturally a lacy animal. Indolence in females. Hybernation. Every young woman ought to be trained to support herself, should necessity require it, and to aid in supporting others. She should, at least, be always industrious. Kinds of labor. Mental labor as truly valuable as bodily.

What ordinary virtue is there more commendable in the young, than industry? On this account, and in this view it is, that well disposed parents sometimes employ their children in a way not absolutely, or in itself, useful to them, for the sake of the general habit. Such parents are certainly excusable, even if their example should not be regarded as commendable, or as worthy of being followed.

Dr. Good, the well known theological, philosophical and medical writer, avows the belief that man is naturally lazy; that he would not so much as lift a finger if he could help it; and that all his activity grows out of a desire to avoid present or future suffering, or pain. Perhaps this is carrying the matter rather too far; since we see young children positively active, not so much from the desire of avoiding pain, as from that of procuring pleasure. But however untrue it may be in regard to children, it is unquestionably true of many adults; and of some, it is to be feared, of both sexes.

Of all lazy persons, however, I dislike most to see a lazy young woman. Destined by her Creator at once to charm, instruct and improve the world around her, by her looks, her words and her actions—and this to a degree which no female has ever yet attained—how exceedingly painful is it to see her floating along the stream of inaction or insignificance, without making one considerable effort to arouse her faculties— bodily, mental and moral—from their half dormant condition.

Too many females who are trained in the bosom of ease and abundance, have no idea of any attempts at benevolent effort, or even of active, untiring industry. If they are not more selfish than the other sex, they are scarcely less so. They live but for themselves, and seem to desire no more. Granting, as we sometimes do, that this is the fault of their education, is it therefore the less pitiable?

I have already urged the importance of self-dependence. Every healthy young woman ought to be so trained, as to be able to make her own way through the world without becoming at all its debtor. I speak now not merely of her moral, and intellectual, and domestic efforts, but also of her physical ones. I care not what her rank or condition may be; every American young woman ought to be able, in the common language of the community; to support herself through life.

I must insist on even more than this. She ought to be able, in point of bodily efficiency, to do something for the support of others; and not merely something, but a great deal. I am not ignorant of the low rate of female wages—disproportioned, altogether so, to their comparative value in the scale of human happiness. And yet, with all necessary abatements, I hold that all healthy females ought to be able to support themselves, should necessity require it, and to aid in supporting others.

Whether, however, their labor supports themselves, or more than does it, is not so much the question, as whether they are truly industrious.

An aged woman, who at ninety was often found at her spinning wheel, and always at active employment—though by no means indigent—was accustomed to say, that every person ought to strain every nerve to get property as long as life lasts, as a matter of duty. I would not say quite so much as this; but I do say that every person, no matter what may be her rank or circumstances, ought to be industrious, from early life to the last moment. Such a person, male or female, will seldom want means of support, and even of distributing "to him that needeth;" but should such a thing happen, it is of no very great importance. She will at least die with the consciousness of having spent her life in active industry, and of having benefited somebody, though she may have spent less on herself.

As to the kind of labor or exercise in which females ought to engage, I have perhaps said enough already. I will only add, that I consider a person as industrious, and as truly worthy of reward—I mean pecuniary reward—in performing valuable mental or moral labor a part of her time, as she who is engaged the whole time with her hands; and I know of no propriety in the custom which has led to the valuation of things by a different standard. I know of no reason, for example, why a young woman who, as a sister, or as a daughter, or as a friend merely, contributes, by wise management, to keep an aged parent or an infant child, or any other person, happy—though it were only by cheerful conversation, or by relating stories fore an hour or so, occasionally—I know not, I say, why she is not as truly entitled to the rewards of industry, as though she were employed in furnishing bread or clothing to the same persons. Are the affections, and passions, and knowledge, and excellence, of less value than the rewards of manual labor, in money or property? And is not mental or spiritual labor at least as valuable as bodily?

CHAPTER XXIII.

VISITING.

Is there no time for relaxation? May there not be passive enjoyments? Passive enjoyments sometimes wrong. How Christian visits should be conducted. Duty and pleasure compatible. Passive visits useful to childhood. Folly of morning calls and evening parties. Bible doctrine of visiting Abuse of visiting.

But is a young woman to be always actively employed? Is not time to be allotted her for mere passive enjoyments? May she never unbend her mind from what is called duty? May she never lay herself, as it were, on the bosom of her family and friends? May she never seat herself on the living green, amid roses and violets, or on the mossy bank studded with cresses or cowslips, and laved by the crystal stream? May she never view the silver fish as he leaps up, and "dumbly speaks the praise of God?" May she never wander abroad for the sake of wandering, or ride for the sake of riding; or gaze on the blue ethereal by day, or the star-spangled canopy by night?

Far be it from me to say any such thing; for I know not to whom such exercises, *as such exercises merely*, may or may not be necessary. That they may be useful to many, cannot be doubted; but that they are far from being useful, or even innocent, to *all*, is quite as certain.

It is certain, I say, that mere passive exercises are not only unnecessary with many, but sometimes wrong. The young woman who is trained, or who has commenced training herself, on truly Christian principles, and who enjoys a tolerable measure of health, will hardly find special seasons of this sort necessary or desirable. She will find sufficient relaxation amid the routine of active life and her daily occupations, and in her labors of love and charity.

The society, of sisters, brothers, parents, grand-parents—of companions, indeed, of every sort with whom she mingles, at home or at school—will afford her, at times, every enjoyment, even of the passive sort, which she really needs; or which, if she has the true spirit of Christ, she will heartily desire. In her duties to these—nay, even in her very duties to herself—in the kitchen, the garden or the field, she will have ample opportunity of descanting on the beauties and glories of the animal and vegetable world, and on the wonders of the starry heavens. In pruning, and watering, and weeding the vines and plants, she may drink in as much as she pleases of the living green, as well as feast her eyes, anon, on the blue expanse; and in her walks of charity and mercy, whether alone or in company with others, she may also receive the nectar of heaven, as it glistens and invites from Nature's own cup, in as rich draughts as if she were merely lounging, and seeking for pleasure—nay, even in richer ones, by as much as active exercise of body and mind, gives her the better mental and physical appetite.

It is one of the strongest proofs that we have a benevolent Creator at the head of the world in which we live, that he has made duty and enjoyment perfectly compatible, so that in pursuing the pathway of the former, we almost inevitably make sure of the latter; and it is also equally remarkable, if not an equally strong proof of benevolence, that in seeking enjoyment, as such, without seeking it in the path of duty, we seldom find it—or if found, it is but half enjoyed.

There is nothing in this world—or hardly any thing, to say the least—which should be done for the mere sake of doing it. We labor not for the sake of laboring, alone; we eat not, and we drink not, for the sake, merely, of eating and drinking—at least we should not, would we obtain the whole benefit of eating and drinking; nor should we even amuse ourselves for the sake alone of the amusement. Double ends are often secured by single means; nay, almost always so. I speak now of the woman, and not of the infant or the child.

Social visits among friends and neighbors, for the mere sake of the passive enjoyment they afford in the earliest years of infancy, may do exceedingly well as a preparation for the more active and more truly Christian visits of maturer years and later life. They are useful in elevating ourselves and others to a state where such visiting is not so needful to our happiness.

As to many forms of visiting current among us—such as morning calls, evening parties, and calls of any sort which answer none of the real purposes of visiting—tending neither to make ourselves or any body else wiser or better, but, on the contrary, to make society worse, indirectly—I have never found any apology for them which seemed to me sufficient to satisfy a rational, intelligent, immortal spirit. To come together late in the evening, just to eat and drink together that which ought not to be eaten and drunk at all—or if at all, certainly not at such an hour; to hold conversation an hour or two under the influence of some sort of excitement, physical or moral, got up for the occasion, on topics which are of little comparative importance—of which the most valuable part often is, the inquiry, How do you do? and the consequent replies to it; to trifle the time away till ten, eleven or twelve o'clock, and then go home through the cold, damp atmosphere, perhaps thinly clad, to suffer that night for want of proper and sufficient sleep, and the next day from indigestion, and a thousand other evils; what can be more truly pitiable, not to say ridiculous! Nor is the practice of putting on a new dress—or one which, if not new, we are quite willing to exhibit—and of going to see our neighbors, and staying just long enough to ask how they do, say a few stale or silly things, and prove an interruption and a nuisance, and then going elsewhere—a whit more justifiable, in beings made in the image of God, and who are to be accountable at his eternal bar.

Let it not be said that I disapprove of visiting, entirely. One of the grounds of condemnation at the final day, is represented in the twenty-fifth chapter of Matthew, as being—"Ye visited me not;" that is, did not visit in the name and for the sake of the Judge, those whom God has made it a duty no less than a privilege to visit. And can I set myself, with impunity, against that which my Saviour has encouraged, and yet pretend to be one of his followers? What would be more presumptuous? I am not an enemy to visiting, if done with a view to glorify God in the benefit of mankind. Let young women visit, indeed, but lot it be done in a way which will be approved by the Saviour and Judge. But there may be dissipation in the garb of visiting; and it is still oftener nothing more than the garb of indolence.

It is not visiting, but visiting without a definite or important purpose, to which I object. It is not visiting itself, but the abuse of visiting. Celestial spirits, for aught we know, are much employed in visiting—and shall not man be so? Are we to belong to their society hereafter, and yet not be their *associates?* Are we to associate with them, and yet remain solitaries? Could such a thing be? Is not man, here and hereafter— as I have already insisted—a social being? And if so, shall not his social nature and social powers be early and successfully developed and cultivated? Let our visits but promote the purposes of benevolence, and nothing can, with propriety, be said against them. I would wage no war on this point, except with selfishness.

CHAPTER XXIV.

MANNERS.

Miss Sedgwick on good manners. Her complaint. Just views of good manners. Good manners as the natural accompaniment of a good heart. The Bible the best book on manners. Illustrations of the subject.

Miss Sedgwick, in her "Means and Ends," has treated the subject of Manners in a happier way than any other writer with whom I am acquainted. Perhaps her views are already familiar to most of my readers; but lest they should not be so, and on account of their excellency, I propose to give a brief abstract of some of them.

She complains, in the first place, that manners are too often considered as certain forms to be taught, or certain modes of conduct for which rules are to be made: and observes that some of the Greek states maintained professors to teach manners; in connection with which she immediately adds the following paragraph:

"Is this making manners a distinct branch of education consistent with their nature? Are they not the sign of inward qualities—a fitting expression of the social virtues? Are they not a mirror which often does, and always should, reflect the soul? For instance, is not a person of mild temper, gentle in manners? Has not another a bold and independent disposition, a forward and fearless manner? It has been well said, that real elegance of demeanor springs from the mind; fashionable schools do but teach its imitation."

Here she quotes, with apparent approbation, the views of Mr. Locke. This writer, in speaking of the moral education of a young person, has the following paragraph:

"If his tender mind be filled with veneration for his parents and teachers, which consists in love and esteem, and a fear to offend them, and with respect and good will to all people, that respect will of itself teach *those ways* which he observes to be most acceptable."

Miss Sedgwick also makes the following judicious remarks:

"I pray you to bear in mind, that manners are but manifestations of character. I must premise that by manners I do not mean the polished manners of the most highly educated and refined of other countries, nor the deferential subservience of their debased classes—so pleasing to those who prefer the homage to the friendship of their fellow creatures.

"Manners, like every thing else in one's character and conduct, should be based on religion. Honor all men, says the apostle. This is the spring of good manners. It strikes at the very root of selfishness. It is the principle by which we render to all ranks and ages their due. A respect for your fellow beings, a reverence for them as God's creatures and our brethren, will inspire that delicate regard to their rights and feelings, of which good manners is the sign.

"If you have truth—not the truth of policy, but religious truth—your manners will be sincere. They will have earnestness, simplicity and frankness—the best qualities of manners. They will be free from assumption, pretence, affectation, flattery and obsequiousness, which are all incompatible with sincerity. If you have a goodly sincerity, you will choose to appear no other nor better than you are—to dwell in a true light."

I have often insisted that the Bible contains the only rules necessary in the study of politeness—or in other words, that those who are the real disciples of Christ, cannot fail to be truly polite. Nor have I any reason for recalling this opinion; from which that of Miss Sedgwick does not materially differ.

Not that the same forms will be observed by every follower of Christ, in manifesting his politeness; all I insist on is, that every one will be truly polite. Let me illustrate my views in a very plain manner.

Suppose a wandering female, clad in the meanest apparel, calls at a house, to inquire the way to the next inn, having just found the road to divide or fork in, a very doubtful and difficult manner. Suppose there are no persons in the house, but half a dozen females. These, we will also suppose, are persons of real piety and true benevolence. What does true politeness require of them, but to give the stranger, in a gentle and affectionate manner, the necessary information?

But if every one is ready to perform the office which true politeness would dictate—and is consequently truly polite—there will probably be as many ways of manifesting these feelings, as there are individuals present in the company.

One, for example, will give the stranger the best directions she can without leaving the room; but will be in all respects exceedingly particular. Another will go to the door, and there give the same directions. A third will go with her into the street, and there instruct her. A fourth will go with her to the first or second fork of the road, and there give further directions. A fifth will send a boy with her. A sixth will sketch the road plainly, though coarsely, with a pencil; and mark, in a proper manner, the course she ought to pursue. Each one will instruct her in an intelligent manner, so that there can hardly remain the possibility of a mistake; but we see that there will be a considerable difference in the form.

It may be said in reply to this view of politeness, that there are genuine disciples of Christ, who, from ignorance of what they ought to do, or from bad habits not yet subdued, will not in such a case as I have described, render any assistance at all; and that they cannot, of course, be truly polite. To which I have only to reply, that such a thing can hardly happen; and if it should, the spirit of Christianity would not lead to it—but it would be the result, rather, of a want of that spirit.

In short, let the young woman who would be truly polite, take her lessons, not in the school of a hollow, heartless world, but in the school of Jesus Christ. I know this counsel may be despised by the gay and fashionable; but it will be much easier to despise it than to prove it to be incorrect.

"Always think of the good of the whole, rather than of your own individual convenience," says Mrs. Farrar, in her Young Ladies' Friend: a most excellent rule, and one to which I solicit your earnest attention. She who is thoroughly imbued with the gospel spirit, will not fail to do so. It was what our Saviour did continually; and I have no doubt that his was the purest specimen of good manners, or genuine politeness, the world has ever witnessed—the politeness of Abraham himself not excepted.

CHAPTER XXV.

HEALTH AND BEAUTY.

Dr. Bell's new work on Health and Beauty. Its value. Adam and Eve probably very beautiful. Primitive beauty of our race to be yet restored. Sin the cause of present ugliness. Never too late to reform. Opinion of Dr. Rush. An important principle. The doctrine of human perfectibility disavowed. Various causes of ugliness. Obedience to law, natural and moral, the true source of beauty. Indecency and immorality of neglecting cleanliness.

Dr. Bell, of Philadelphia, whose reputation as a medical man and an author is deservedly high, has written a volume, as the reader may already know, entitled, "Health and Beauty"—in which he endeavors to show that "a pleasing contour, symmetry of form, and a graceful carriage of the body," may be acquired, and "the common deformities of the spine and chest be prevented," by a due obedience to the "laws of growth and exercise." These laws he has endeavored—and with considerable success—to present in a popular and intelligible manner.

Nor was the task unworthy the efforts and pen of the gifted individual by whom it was executed. Young women, of course, are inclined to set a high value on beauty of form and feature, as well as to dread, more than most other persons, what they regard as deformity. Surely they ought to be glad of a work like that I have described.

I have no wish to disparage beauty; it is almost a virtue. There can hardly be a doubt that Adam and Eve were exceedingly beautiful; nor that so far as the world can be restored to its primitive state—which we hope may be the case in its future glorious ages—the pristine beauty of our race will be restored. It is sin, in the largest sense of the term, which has distorted the human "face divine," disrobed it of half its charms; and deprived the whole frame of its symmetry.

Does any one ask, of what possible service it can be to know these facts, when it is too late to make use of them? The truth is, it can never be too late. There is no person so old that she cannot improve her appearance, more or less, if she will but take the appropriate steps. I do not, of course, mean to say, that at twenty or thirty years of age a person can greatly alter the contour of the face, or the symmetry of the frame; though I believe some thing can be done, even in these respects. It was the saying of Dr. Rush, that husbands and wives who live happily together, always come to resemble one another more and more, in their very features; and he accounted for it on the principle of an increased resemblance in their feelings, tastes or dispositions. And there are probably few who have not observed how much bad passions and bad habits distort the features of every body, at every age. Then why should not Dr. Rush be right; and why should not good feelings and good affections change the countenance, in a greater or less degree, as well as bad ones? And what reason, then, can be given why every young woman—certainly those who are far down in the column of *teens*—cannot change her countenance for the better, if she will take the necessary pains for it?

That she can do but little, is no reason why that little should not be done. The very consideration that she can do but little, enhances the importance of doing what she can. Let her remember this. Would that the principle were universally remembered and applied! Would that it were generally believed—and the belief acted upon—that the latter day glory of the world is to be brought about in no other way than by having every individual of every generation, through a long series of generations, do all in his power, aided by wisdom and strength from on high, to hasten it.

Do not suppose that I entertain the belief, as foolish as it is absorb, that in any future glorious period of the world's history, mankind will be perfectly beautiful, or perfectly conformed to one standard of beauty. I entertain no belief in human perfectibility. I believe—and I wish to state this belief once for all, that I may not be misunderstood—that we are destined, if we are wise, to approach perfection forever, without the possibility of ever attaining to it;—to any perfection, I mean, which is absolute and unqualified.

Nor do I believe that all mankind will ever become perfectly beautiful, according to any particular standard of beauty. This were neither useful nor desirable. There will probably be as great a variety of features, and possibly, too, of size and symmetry, in the day of millennial glory, as there is now.

What I believe, is this. That in falling, with our first parents, we fall physically as well as morally; and that our physical departure from truth is almost as wide as our moral. I suppose all the ugliness of the young—not, of course, all their variety of feature or complexion, but all which constitutes real ugliness of appearance—comes directly or indirectly from the transgression of God's laws, natural or moral; and can only be restored by obedience to those laws by the transgression of which it came.

It is not tight dressing alone which spoils the shape; but improper exercise, neglect of exercise, over exercise—and a thousand other things also. Nor is it the application of *rouge* alone, which spoils the beauty. There are a thousand physical transgressions that dim the lustre of the eye, or sink it too deep in the socket, or flatten it, or paint a circle round it. So of the face in general. There are a thousand forms of transgression that take away the carnation of the lip and cheek, and leave unnatural hues, not to say pimples and furrows, in its stead.

I might be much more particular. I might show how every physical transgression—every breach of that part of the natural law which imposes on us the duty of proper attention to cleanliness, exercise, dress, air, temperature, eating, drinking, sleeping, &c.—mars, in a greater or less degree, our beauty. Such a disclosure might be startling; but it ought to be made. Dr. Bell, in the volume mentioned, has led the way; and his work entitles him to a high place among the benefactors of our race. But he has only begun the work; the important honor of completing it, remains to him, or to some of his countrymen.

But enough on this subject, for the present, if I have convinced the reader whence her help, in this respect, is to come;—if I have convinced her that, under God, she is to restore her beauty only by becoming a true Christian; by having her whole being—body, intellect and affections—brought into subjection to divine law, especially by a prompt, and minute, and thorough obedience to all the laws of health and life, as far as she understands them; and by diligent effort to understand them better and better, as long as she lives; and, lastly, by the smiles of Almighty God upon her labors and efforts.

CHAPTER XXVI.

NEATNESS AND CLEANLINESS.

Reasons for discussing these topics. Every person should undergo a thorough ablution once a day. Quotation from Mrs. Farrar. Two important objects gained by cold bathing. Its value as an exercise. Various forms of bathing. Philosophy of this subject. Vast amount of dirt accumulating on the surface. Statement of Mr. Buckingham Bathing necessary in all employments. Offices of the skin, and evil consequences of keeping it in an uncleanly condition.

After saying so much of the general importance of obeying the laws of life and health, it seems, at first view, almost unnecessary to go farther into particulars than I have already done And yet I feel somewhat inclined to do so for two reasons. First, because I find several considerable errors in the advice given to young women in some of our young women's books, in matters pertaining to their physical improvement, which I should rejoice to be able to correct. Secondly, because, that in a work from me, information of this kind will probably be expected.

And yet it seems quite common-place to advise a young woman on the subject of cleanliness in general; and still more so, to speak to her on the subject of personal neatness. A young woman wanting in neatness! At the first view of the case, such a thing seems almost impossible.

Would that it were so! Would that our daughters and sisters—the daughters and sisters of America, especially—were so far apprized of this indispensable requisite, as to need no monitor on the subject! But, unhappily, it is not so. Very far from it, on the contrary.

No person in tolerable health, male or female, seems to me to be entitled to be considered as neat—truly so—who does not wash the surface of the whole body in water, daily. But are there not multitudes who pass for models of neatness and cleanliness, who do not perform this work for themselves half a dozen times—nay, once—a year?

That I may not be regarded as wholly ultra on this subject, because professedly a strong friend and advocate of physical education and physical improvement, I beg leave to subjoin the following paragraphs from Mrs. Farrar's Young Ladies' Friend:

"Once, at least, in twenty-four hours, the whole surface of the body should be washed in soap and water, and receive the friction of a coarse towel, or flesh brush, or crash mitten. This may be done by warm or cold bathing; by a plunging or shower bath; by means of a common wash tub; and even without further preparation than an ordinary wash-bowl and sponge.

"By washing a small part of the person at a time, rubbing it well, and then covering what is done, the whole may be washed in cold water, even in winter time; and a glow may be produced after it, in a young and healthy person.

"It is common for persons who are in the habit of sponging over with cold water every morning, or of taking the shower or plunging bath, to omit it when they have a slight cold, or sore throat, or a touch of rheumatism; whereas, if it were properly done so as to produce a glow all over the skin, their habitual ablutions would be the best remedy for the beginnings of evil. * * * If not sure, in such a case, of producing a glow after the use of the cold water, it will be better to use the warm, in order to make the skin do its office freely. But to cease your customary bathing at such times, is to increase all your difficulties.

"Many think it impossible to make this thorough washing when the weather is very cold, and that they must do it in rooms never warmed by a fire; but in healthy and vigorous persons, the glow after washing would be so great, as to more than compensate for the momentary chill."

By washing the body in cold water every day, and following it by friction, according to the recommendation of Mrs. F., you gain, at once, two important objects. You secure to yourself the benefits of cleanliness, and of a vast amount of exercise, and consequent vigor. I say a *vast* amount; but this depends much on yourself. You may make a great deal of it, or only a little. I know of one teacher who says his cold bath and friction are worth two hours of ordinary exercise to him every day. But two hours of ordinary exercise a day, is much more than the whole which is taken by some of our young women.

I have spoken of the vigor derived from cold bathing. This is gained in two ways. First, *directly*, by the action of the muscles or moving powers, which I have partially described in the chapter on Exercise. Secondly, *indirectly*, through the medium of sympathy. I know of no one thing which costs so little time and effort—(for the work may be done after it has become natural and habitual, in twelve or fifteen minutes)—which secures, at the same time, such an amount of exercise and bodily vigor, as daily cold bathing.

The particular forms of bathing are numerous. Among these, are the simple washing with the hand, spoken of by Mrs. Farrar; sponging; immersion in a tub or stream; and the shower bath. All these, except, of course, washing in a stream, may be done with cold, tepid, warm or hot water; and may be continued for a greater or less time—although, in general, the cold bath should be a quick operation.

Let me now present the reader with a physiological explanation of the use and necessity of frequent ablution and bathing; derived, in substance, from a little tract already before the public. [Footnote: See "Thoughts on Bathing." page 8.] I use the language of the tract, because I can use none which is better for my present purpose.

The dust accumulates on the surface of our bodies much more readily, and adheres much more firmly, and in much larger quantities, than is usually supposed, and than by many would be credited. Mr. Buckingham, the Oriental traveller, asserts that from two to three pounds of it are sometimes removed from the whole surface of a person who has for some time neglected bathing and washing, in a tropical climate; and this, under some circumstances, may possibly have been the case. For not only does the moisture of the skin favor its accumulation, but so also does the oily substance continually poured out by the small bottle-shaped glands—sebaceous glands, as they are called—which are found in the skin in great numbers, with their mouths opening on its surface.

Nothing, indeed, can be more obvious to an enlightened and reflecting mind, than the indispensable necessity of frequent ablutions of the body in some form or other. It will, indeed, be said—it is often said—that much depends, in this respect, upon the nature of our occupation. The farmer, the smith, the manufacturer—the individual, in one word, whose employment is most uncleanly—will be thought to need frequent attentions of this kind, while those whose employments are quiet and sedentary, will need them less frequently.

But it should not be forgotten, that although frequent bathing and cleansing are indispensable to those whose employments expose them to a great deal of dust, yet they are scarcely less necessary to the sedentary; and for the following reason:—The active nature of the employments of the former, and their exposure to the open air, break up the coating of oil and dirt with which they are enveloped, and render it more pervious to the matter of perspiration, than the thinner, but not less tenacious varnish which covers the surface of the sedentary. On the whole, therefore, I regard bathing and thorough cleansing of the skin, as of nearly equal importance in all the varied circumstances of age, sex, climate and occupation.

We must not omit to observe, that whatever changes take place in the lungs, by the action of the air upon the blood in the small vessels of those organs, to purify and renovate it, take place all over the surface of the body; that in this respect, therefore, the skin may be regarded as a sort of appendage to the lungs; and that if the skin he varnished over with a mixture of oil and dust, so that it cannot perform its office, an unreasonable burden will be thrown upon the lungs, which will thereby be weakened, and predisposed to disease. I have not a doubt, that a universal neglect of cleanliness not only favors, in this way, the production of lung diseases—especially of those colds which are so frequent in our climate, and which often pave the way for other and still more dangerous diseases—but also that it tends to aggravate such diseases of the lungs as may already exist, or to whose existence there may be in us, either by inheritance or otherwise—a predisposition.

This temporary suspension of the offices of the skin is, however, peculiarly dangerous to those who are of light complexion, slender form, with a long neck, and narrow shoulders projecting almost like wings—indicating a chest whose internal organs, as well as external dimensions, are comparatively small and feeble, and therefore poorly prepared to do that work which belongs to other parts or organs. Let all persons beware of compelling the lungs *to work for the skin*; but above all, those who have the particular structure to which I have alluded.

It is hardly necessary that I should advert, here, to the repugnance felt by our sex, to those young women whose external appearance bespeaks a want of attention to this subject. But it is necessary that I should allude to the indecency of that neglect—by no means uncommon—which renders the odor of the perspiration very disagreeable, or increases its disagreeableness by means of accumulations of grease and dirt on the skin.

They should also be reminded that there is, somehow or other, (I know not how, exactly,) a very general connection between external and internal purity. It is exceedingly uncommon—I had almost said, quite so—to find an individual who pays a daily close attention to neatness and cleanliness of person and dress, who does not, at the same time, possess a reputation which is not only above reproach, but also quite above suspicion.

CHAPTER XXVII.

Legitimate purposes of dress—as a covering, a regulator of temperature, and a defence. Use of ornaments. Further thoughts on dress. How clothing keeps us warm. Errors in regard to the material, quality, and form of our dress. Tight lacing—its numerous evils. Improvement of the lungs by education. Objections to the use of personal ornaments.

When we remember that the threefold object of dress is to cover, warm and defend us, and that the kind and quantity of dress which best does this, is most conducive to our own and the public good, as well as to the glory of God, we are led, very naturally, to the following reflections:

1. We have no right to use that kind of dress which does not answer well the purpose of a COVERING, ad long as we can lawfully obtain that which would do it better. All fashions, moreover, which tend to remind the beholder that our dress is *designed as a covering*, are nearly as improper as those which do not effectually cover us.

And here let me say, with sufficient plainness, that there are such fashions in existence; and that they ought to be shunned like the plague. Does not the world in which we live, contain sources enough of temptation, and avenues enough to vice, seduction and misery, without increasing their number by our dress? [Footnote: I cannot refrain from saying, in this place, that since I wrote the above paragraph, I have received an excellent letter from a worthy minister of the gospel, on the subject of female dress which, besides greatly confirming the views I have expressed in this chapter, suggests the importance of having a standard dress devised—to be formed on Christian principles, and made fashionable by Christian example. If such a measure is desirable, it is yours, young women, to put it in operation.]

I need to specify but one fashion in the list of those to which I refer. It is the fashion of exposing the neck and a part of the chest. I could tell young women, that it would be wisdom to remove this dangerous custom, were health entirely out of the question. A word to the wise—to adopt the language of Solomon—is sufficient. May it prove so, in the present instance. Let not the young of the other sex, miseducated as they now are, and the slaves of improper imaginations and feelings, be longer trifled with in this matter.

2. We have no right to use any articles of clothing-when we have it in our power, by lawful means, to prevent it—whose tendency is directly contrary to what has been laid down as the second great object of dress, that of ASSISTING TO KEEP OUR BODIES AT A PROPER TEMPERATURE.

It would be idle to pretend that clothing, in itself considered, is a source of warmth to our bodies. It is only so by the relation it bears to our bodies; or, in other words, by the circumstances in which it is placed. Our own bodies—their internal, living machinery, rather—are the principal sources of our heat. Clothing is useful in keeping us warm, only by retaining, for some time, a portion of the heat of our bodies, which would otherwise escape so rapidly into the ambient cooler air, as to leave us with a sensation of chilliness. It should, therefore, be adapted to the season. That clothing which conducts the heat from the body in the slowest manner, or, in other words, impedes most its progress, is best adapted to severe cold weather; provided, however, it does not keep the heated air in contact with the body so long as to render it impure. And, on the contrary, that clothing which most readily allows the heat to escape from our bodies, is, in hot weather, the best adapted to our health and happiness.

I have said that the internal machinery of out bodies is the great source of our heat. Foremost, perhaps, in this work, are the lungs, the stomach, the brain and nervous system, and the circulatory system, including the heart, arteries, veins and absorbents. Our moving powers—the muscles and tendons—have, indeed, much to do with generating our heat; but it is principally by the assistance which they render to the digestive, the nutritive, the respiratory, the circulatory, and the thinking machinery. The fat of our bodies has also something to do in promoting our warmth; but it is only on the same principle as that by which it is done by our clothing; that is to say, it prevents the heat from being conducted off too rapidly.

All these internal organs—and, in fact, all the living machinery of our bodies—have the power to generate heat and diffuse it over the system, in proportion to the freedom and energy of their action; or, to express the same idea in fewer words, in proportion to their health.

But this is not all. They have not only the power of generating heat in proportion to their healthiness, but also of resisting cold. Who does not know that the living system, at ninety-eight degrees of Fahrenheit, will resist a temperature nearly one hundred and fifty degrees lower than this, [Footnote: During the present winter, the mercury in this vicinity has ranged, in one or two instances, as low as 14 or 16 degrees below zero; which is 112 or 114 degrees below the heat of the blood. In some parts of New England it has been 20 or 30 degrees below.] and yet for some time not freeze? Perhaps this is done, however, in the same way in which a more moderate amount of heat is generated. Perhaps the increased muscular and nervous energy, and the increased activity of the other organs, enable them to generate heat as fast, as the increased cold around carries it off.

But the conclusion. I would at present enforce from these physiological premises, is the following:—That whenever our dress, by means of its material, form or quantity, has a tendency to weaken our internal organs, or any one of them, and thus to prevent the free and energetic performance of their several functions, it is injurious, and its use is wrong, not to say sinful.

This is sometimes done by clothing which irritates and excites the surface of the body too much. Coarse flannel is more irritating than any other material in ordinary use, and should therefore never be used when a sufficient amount of bodily heat can be maintained without it; as its use weakens, in the end, the perspiratory, and calorific, and depurating powers of the skin—for the skin has all these powers—and even, in some cases, brings on eruptive and other diseases. Fine flannel is more irritating than cotton; and the latter, more so than linen. Still, there are multitudes who cannot get along without flannel, at some seasons, either coarser or finer.

The evil of which I have spoken is, however, much oftener induced by error in regard to the quantity of dress, than its quality. As to quantity, we need no more than is just necessary, along with healthy and vigorous exercise, to keep us from being sensibly cold or chilly. Any amount beyond this, be its nature what it may, is debilitating, and consequently more or less injurious.

But the form of our dress often does injury; as well as its material and quantity. With some classes of our community, this is a greater evil than either of the former; though with others, it is not.

All forms of dress which impede any kind of motion, especially those which impede circulatory motion, are greatly injurious. It is, I suppose, pretty well known, that all parts of the skin are full of minute blood vessels, chiefly veins; in addition to which, there are also a great number of veins still larger, immediately under the skin, and connected with it, as may be observed by looking at the hands or limbs of very aged or very lean persons. Now the tendency or course of the blood in all the veins, is towards the heart; and this course is slower or more rapid, according as the skin is more or less active, healthy and free. A rapid course of the blood in these veins, is desirable, because it has become, in the progress of its circulation, greatly impure, and in the same proportion unfit to minister to the purposes of health—and needs to go on to the heart, and through that to the lungs, to be relieved of its load of impurities.

Is it not plain, then, that all compression of the skin by cravats, wristbands, waistbands, belts, garters, or any other form of ligatures, must be wrong! Must it not impede the motion of the venous blood in its return to the heart? Must not even light boots, garters, stockings, &c., do this? Is it not a task sufficiently difficult for the blood to climb from the feet to the heart, directly against the power of gravity, without being impeded, is its course, by compression of any sort—and above all, by ligatures.

But if these ordinary compressions of the surface of our bodies are so injurious, what are we to say of the practice of many females, and of most young women—at least in fashionable life—of compressing the chest?

For in compressing this part of the frame, though we do not impede the action of *so much* blood in its return to the heart as might be supposed, we do a great deal more injury in many other respects than is usually known. I must advert to the various items of this injury.

First—compressing the chest, by dress or otherwise, prevents free motion of the trunk of the body. We can, indeed, bend the body a little, notwithstanding the compression; but not so freely, and not therefore so healthfully.

Secondly—compression of the chest prevents the lungs and heart—the principal organs wholly contained in its cavity—from expanding, and doing their work in a proper manner. If there were no compression by ligatures or otherwise, of any other part of the system, and if the impure blood came back to the lungs for renovation as fast as it ought, still it would not be properly depurated or renovated, unless the lungs acted in a full, healthy and rigorous manner. But this they cannot do, unless the chest is left free from external compression. Their internal expansion and enlargement is limited by the external, much in the same way as the space in a bellows is limited or extended according as the bellows itself is expanded or compressed.

If the muscles concerned in moving the chest—near a hundred in number—do not properly act; if the breast-bone, when we inhale air, is not thrown forward, and the ribs thrown outward and upward so as to increase, very greatly, the size of the internal cavity; then the venous blood which is brought into the lungs to be purified and cleansed, cannot—I repeat it—be purified and cleansed as it ought to be; and the whole system must suffer the consequences, in being fed and nourished on impure, and I might say poisonous blood.

This is the case when the lungs are compressed during a single breath: how great, then, is the evil, when the compression continues an hour—during which period we probably breathe ten or twelve hundred times! How much greater still, when it is continued through the waking hours of a day, say fifteen or sixteen—in which period we breathe nearly twenty thousand times—and a young woman of twelve to fifteen years of age, probably more! But think of the evil as extended to a year, or three hundred and sixty-five days! or to a whole life of thirty, fifty or seventy years!

How much poisoned blood must go through the living system in sixty or seventy years, should the injured system last so long! And how many bad feelings, and how much severe pain and suffering, and chronic and acute disease, must almost inevitably be undergone!

Thirdly—this poisoning of the blood, however, is not all. The chest, so constantly compressed, even if the compression is not begun in early infancy, shrinks to a much smaller size than is natural, and in a few years becomes incapable of holding more than half or two thirds as much air as before; so that if the compression is removed, the injury cannot be wholly restored—though if removed any time before thirty-five years of age, *something* may be done towards restoration. But not only is the cavity diminished permanently in size; the bones and tendons are bent out-of their place, and made to compress either the lungs themselves, or the other contiguous organs, as the heart, the liver and the stomach, and to disturb the proper performance of their respective offices or functions.

Fourthly-tight lacing, as I have already said, compresses the heart as well as the lungs, and impedes the motion of this important organ. The suffering and disease which are thus entailed on transgression, if not quite so great in amount as that which is induced by the abuse of the lungs, is yet very great—and added to the former, greatly diminishes the sum total of human happiness, and increases, in the same proportion, our miseries and our woes.

Fifthly—the stomach is also a sufferer—and the liver; and, indeed, all the other organs. There is suffering, not only from being in actual contact with each other, but also from sympathy and fellow feeling. I have adverted to that law, by which, if one member or organ of the human system suffer, all the others suffer with it. This is very remarkably the case with the lungs, when they suffer. Other organs suffer with them from mere sympathy; and that to a very great extent. This is especially true of the cerebral and nervous system; and of that portion of the *general* system which gives to woman her peculiar prerogative, as well as her distinctive character.

Let no young woman forget, moreover, that she lives, not for herself alone, but for others; and that if she injures health and life by improper dress, she does it not for herself alone, but for all those who shelter their abuses under her example, as well as for all those who may hereafter be more immediately influenced by her present conduct. Let her neither forget her responsibility nor her accountability. Would to God that she could see this matter as it truly is, and as she will be likely to see it in years to come!

Let it be remembered, moreover, that as we can diminish the size of the chest by compressing it, so we can enlarge it, gradually—especially in early life—by extra effort; or by general exercise; but especially such general exercise as I have mentioned in a former chapter—I mean, moderate labor in the garden or in the field, and in house-keeping. Nor is spinning on a high wheel—which requires not only walking to and fro, but also considerable motion of the arms and chest—a very bad exercise. A great deal may also be done by reading aloud in a proper manner, and by conversation; and especially by singing.

I believe that by a proper education of the lungs—instead of the modern custom of _un_educating them—it would be possible, in the course of a few successive ages, greatly to enlarge the cavity containing them. And if this can be done, it will be a means of promoting, in the same degree, the tone and vigor, not only of the lungs themselves, but also of the whole physical frame; and the aggregate gain to our race would be immense. Let us think of the amazing difference between a race which has been deteriorating in body and mind, from generation to generation, and at the same time suffering from disease in a thousand forms, and one which is not only free from primitive disease, but gradually improving, both bodily and mentally, and in a fair way to go on improving for centuries—perhaps thousands of years—to come!

3. We have no right to use that dress as a DEFENCE which does not answer this purpose, so long as we can get that which does; provided it answers neither of the other two purposes already mentioned.

Now, are there not a great number of articles of clothing worn, whose use cannot be justified on these principles? Does not the greater part of human time and labor which is expended on dress, both by the maker and the wearer, go to answer other purposes than these? Is it not expended for mere ornament? And is such an expenditure right?

My own conviction is, that we are bound, as Christians—and as such, I must consider my readers in this favored country—to use that dress, and that alone, which answers the great purposes of dress; and that were the subject viewed in its true and just light, all beyond this should be regarded as sinful. What I suppose these great purposes of dress are, has already been mentioned.

In short, I suppose that our duty is, to dress in such a way, if our circumstances permit it, as will be best for the purposes of merely clothing, tempering and defending our bodies. That material, that quantity, and those forms of dress, which we suppose best accomplish this, should be adopted as fast as they are known.

Such a view will, of course, be opposed by the devotees of fashion; but not, I think, by many of those who know they cannot serve two masters—God and mammon, or God and the fashions—and that it is their duty to devote themselves, unreservedly, to the worship and service of the former.

I shall also be opposed by another class—the devotees of utility, or a species of what I call utilitarianism. They will say that *I* am a utilitarian, of the rankest sort; that I would destroy all just taste, all industry, all division of labor, all commerce, and all wealth.

But is it so? Is that proved to be a just taste, to which the views here presented seem to be opposed? Where is the proof, and by whom has it been adduced? I am no advocate for a utilitarianism which excludes just taste: but *I believe our tastes to be depraved by the fall, no less than our affections;* that they are not, as some suppose, *free from sin*—though less sinful, perhaps, than our moral tastes and preferences. I believe that a taste which is not conformed to the nature of things and to the law of God, is a perverted taste; and that the modern taste in regard to dress and ornament, is, to a great extent, of this description.

And does there remain no room for industry when personal ornaments are excluded? As well might it be said that the exclusion of all drinks but water, would strike a death-blow at industry. Is there nothing left for people to do, because you take away ornament?

Perhaps, indeed, if *all* personal ornament were to be taken away suddenly, it might give a temporary check to industry, and seem to conflict with the principal of a division of labor. But this cannot happen, except it were by miraculous agency. The utmost that can be rationally expected at present by the most sanguine, would be, that professing Christians should exclude it; nor could they, as a body, be expected to do it at once. One here, and another there, would renounce, as wrong, what he had been accustomed to think right; and this would give society time to adjust itself, and preserve its balance; as it has done in the case of every great and important change of public opinion.

But we are gravely told by several writers on this subject, that as a nation's wealth is derived from a division of labor, it follows, that to deny ourselves all ornament, would be a great injury to the community.

What a strange inference! Is there nothing for people to do, in this world, I again ask, but to make ornaments? Or can it be that they form so important a division of human labor, that to dispense with them in the only way in which it is possible, humanly speaking, to do so—that is, by enlightening public opinion, and appealing to the conscientious—is to take away the wealth of the nation?

I deny, most resolutely, that mere artificial ornaments make any considerable part of a nation's real wealth. That which tends to make us healthier in all the functions of our bodies—which developes and improves all the faculties of our minds—and which developes and cultivates, to the highest possible extent, all the good affections of the soul-is alone worthy of the name of wealth.

I do not deny, that he who makes two stalks of grain grow where only one grew before, is a public benefactor. I do not deny that, for certain purposes in the arts—in architecture, especially—he who polishes a gem, or a block of marble, may also be a public benefactor. This is a very different thing from preparing and applying ornaments to our persons; and may be, to some extent, useful. But I am still assured, that those who make a person healthier than before, or improve his intellect, or are a means of awakening in him a love to God and man, and of promoting its growth where it is already awakened, are benefactors to the world in a degree infinitely higher, and add to its *true* riches almost infinitely more.

It is health, knowledge and excellence—we again say—which exalt a nation; and these are its true wealth. Fifteen millions of free men, all as healthy as the most perfect specimen which could now be found among us; all as wise as the wisest man in the world; and all as virtuous and excellent as Aristides, or Howard, or Benezet, or John, the beloved apostle, himself—what a national treasure they would be! what a revenue of true wealth they would afford!

Now, if fifteen millions of such people would be a source of national wealth before unheard of, would not every individual of this whole number be a source of wealth? And would not every element which should go to make up the sum total of the excellences of each individual, be a part of this mighty treasure?

If the richer part of the community have money to spare, why should they not spend it in increasing the health, the knowledge, and the morality of the needy around them—by giving employment to those who are capable of promoting these blessings, and who want employment?

It will be said, I know, that the great multitude of persons around us are not fit for more elevated employments. No; nor will they ever be, in any considerable numbers, until they come to be employed in this way much more frequently than they now are. Let there be an urgent demand in the market for a commodity, and it usually soon comes to be abundant. Let there be a demand for laborers in the mental and moral field—in this more elevated garden of the Lord—and they will, ere long, be furnished; and the more persons there are employed in this way, and who consequently come into the habit of fitting themselves to be thus employed, the richer will be the national treasury.

That many young women, who read this chapter, will wholly lay aside their ornaments, and fit themselves, as fast as possible, for the noble purpose of ornamenting those around them, by promoting their physical, intellectual and moral well being, can hardly be expected. But I do hope that I shall lead a few to expend less of time and money in dressing and ornamenting their persons than heretofore, and more in dressing and ornamenting the immortal mind, as well as more in promoting health of body.

I cannot but hope to live to see the day, when every person who professes the name of Jesus Christ, and not a few who make no professions at all, will entertain similar views in regard to the purposes of dress and their own duty in relation to it, to those which I have endeavored to inculcate. Such a day must surely come, sooner or later; and I hope that those who believe this, will make it their great rule to *expend as little on themselves as possible*, and yet answer the true intentions of the Creator respecting themselves.

There is a very wide difference between spending as *much* as we can on our persons—in the gratification, I mean, of the wants of our depraved tastes, under the specious plea that it encourages commerce and industry—and spending as *little* as we can on ourselves, and as much as possible in promoting the health, the learning, and the piety of ourselves and those around us. The former has been tried for centuries—

with what result, let the state of society and our misnamed refinement bear witness. Let the latter be tried but half as long, and the world will be surprised at the results.

Foremost in this work of reform, should be our millions of young women. They should be so for two reasons. First, because their influence and responsibilities to coming generations are great, and, secondly, because they are at present greatly involved in the practical error of loving external ornaments too well, and of valuing too little the ornaments of a healthy body, a sound mind, and a good heart.

I am often pained to hear the reproach cast upon females, and especially upon the younger of the sex, that they are fond of the "far-fetched" and "dear-bought," even when they are the less valuable. It should not be so. They should be above the suspicion of such a weakness.

What else can be expected, however, when those who should be the guardians of the public taste—and who should, as Christian citizens, strive with all their might to elevate it—engage in pandering to the follies, not to say the depravities, of the age? Let young women rise above themselves, and escape the snares thus laid for them by those who ought to be their guides to the paths of wisdom, and virtue, and happiness.

CHAPTER XXVIII.

DOSING AND DRUGGING.

Tendency of young women to dosing and drugging. "Nervousness." Qualms of the stomach. Eating between our meals—its mischiefs. Evils of direct dosing. What organs are injured. Confectionery. The danger from quacks and quackery.

Fallen as human nature—our physical nature with the rest—now is, there are seasons in the lives of almost all of us, when we are either ill, or fear we shall be so. And young women, as well as others, have their seasons of debility, and their fears, and even their sick days. They have their colds, their coughs, their sick headaches, their indigestions, and their consumptions. Above all—and more frequently by far than almost any thing else—they have those undefinable and indescribable feelings of ennui, which, for want of a better name, are called, in their various forms, "nervousness."

When the unpleasant sensations to which I have just alluded, are referred to the region of the stomach, and only produce a few qualms, young women are not, in general, so apt to take medicine, as to eat something to keep down their bad feelings—as a bit of seed-cake, a little fruit, some cloves or cinnamon, or a piece of sugar.

This, though better than to take medicine, is yet a very bad practice; for although momentary relief is secured in this way, it never fails to increase the unpleasant sensations in the end. I ought to say somewhere—and I know of no better place than this—that the habit of eating between our regular meals, even the smallest thing whatever; is of very mischievous tendency; and this for several reasons. First—the stomach needs its seasons of entire rest; but those persons who eat between their meals seldom give any rest to their stomachs, except during the night. Secondly—eating things in this way injures the general appetite. Thirdly—the habit is apt to increase in strength, and is difficult to break. Fourthly—it does not afford relief, except for a very short time. On the contrary, as I have already intimated, it increases the trouble in the end.

This eating of such simple things, I have said, is quite bad enough; but there are errors which are worse. Such is the habit of taking an extra cup of tea or coffee—extra, either as respects the number of cups or the strength. Now tea and coffee-and sometimes either of them—are very apt to afford, like eating a little food, a temporary relief. Indeed, the sufferer often gains so long a respite from her sufferings, that the narcotic beverage which she takes is supposed to be the very medicine needed, and the very one adapted to her case. The like erroneous conclusion is often made after using, with the same apparent good effect, certain hot herb teas. Yet, I repeat it, such medicinal mixtures usually—perhaps I should say always— aggravate the complaint in the end, by deranging still more the powers and functions of the stomach, and debilitating still more the cerebral and nervous system.

Different and various are the external applications made to the head, in these circumstances; but all, usually, with the same success; they only produce a little temporary relief. The same may be said of the use of smelling bottles—containing, as I believe they usually do, ammonia or hartshorn, cologne water, camphor, &c. The manner in which these operate to produce mischief, is, however, very different from that of the former. They irritate the nasal membrane, and dry it, if they do not slowly destroy its sensibility. They also, in some way, affect seriously the tender brain. In any event, they ought seldom to be used by the sick or the well. Nor is this all. They are *inhaled*—to irritate and injure the lining membrane of the lungs.

Trifling as it may seem to many, I never find that a young woman keeps a cologne bottle in her dressing room, or a smelling bottle about her—or perfumes her clothes—or is in the habit of eating, every now and then, a little coriander, or fennel, or cloves, or cinnamon—without trembling for her safety. Persisting long in this habit, she will as inevitably injure her brain and nervous system, her lungs or her stomach— ay, and her teeth too—as she continues the habit. I never knew a young woman who had used any of these things, year after year, for a long series of years, whose system was not already suffering therefrom; and if I were fond of giving or receiving challenges, I should not hesitate to challenge the whole world to produce a single instance of the kind. In the very nature of things it cannot be. Such persons may tell us they are well, when we make an attack upon their habits; but take them when off their guard, and we hear, at times, quite a different story.

In regard to the daily, or even the occasional use of the stronger drugs of the apothecary's shop—whether this *shop* is found in the family or elsewhere—I would fain hope many of our young women may claim an entire immunity. It seems to me to be enough, that they should spoil their breath, their skin, their stomachs and their nerves, with perfumes, aromatic seeds and spices, confectionary, and the like, without adding thereto the more active poisons—as laudanum, camphor, picra, antimony, &c.

The mention of the word confectionary, in the last paragraph, brings to my mind a congregated host of evils which befall young women, as the legitimate consequences of its use. Some may suppose that the class of young women for whom I am writing, have little to do with confectionary; that they have risen above it. Would that it were so! But that it is not, many a teacher of young ladies' boarding schools, female seminaries, &c.—to say nothing of parents—might abundantly testify.

That they are very often the dupes of the quacks and quackery with which our age abounds—or at least, that they take many of the pills, and cough drops, and bitters, and panaceas of the day—I will not believe. Much as they err to their own destruction, I trust they have not yet sunk so low as this.

CHAPTER XXIX.

TAKING CARE OF THE SICK.

The art of taking care of the sick should be a part of female education. Five reasons for this. Doing good. Doing good by proxy. Great value of personal services. How can young women be trained to these services? Contagion. Breathing bad air. Aged nurses. Scientific instruction of nurses. Visiting and taking care of the sick, a religious duty. Appeal to young women.

The art of taking care of the sick, should be considered an indispensable part of female education. Some of the reasons for this are the following:

1. As society now is, there is danger that the number of our young women who fall into a state of indifference, not to say absolute disgust, with the world and with life, will greatly increase, unless the sex can be led, by an improved course of education, to exercise more of that active sympathy with suffering which prompts to assist in relieving it.

2. Nurses of the sick are greatly needed. It not unfrequently happens, that good nurses cannot be obtained, male or female, except by going very far in search for them. And yet it would seem that every one must know the *importance* of good nurses, from the prevalence of the maxim—not more prevalent than just— "A good nurse is worth as much as a physician."

What physician has not, again and again, seen all his efforts fail to do any good, because not sustained by the labors of a skilful, intelligent, faithful and persevering nurse? This condition is one of the most trying that can befall him; and yet, trying as it is, it is his very frequent lot.

3. Females are better qualified—other things being the same—for attending the sick, than males. They not only have a softer hand, and more kindness and gentleness, but they are also more devoted to whatever they undertake; and they have more fortitude in scenes of trial and distress. Their thoughts are, moreover, less engrossed by the cares of business, and by other objects, than those of our sex. They seem formed for days, and months, and years of watchfulness—not only over our earliest infancy, but also over our first and second childhood. And it were strange indeed, if nature, in qualifying them for all this, had not qualified them to watch over us during the few short years that intervene.

There may, indeed, be instances—there certainly are some such—where the physical strength of females, unaided, is not sufficient for the task of which I am speaking. For the most part, however, it is gentleness, and patience, and fortitude, which are most wanted and in these, woman stands pre-eminent.

4. It is often advantageous to have female assistance in taking care of the sick, because it can be afforded at a much lower rate than that of males. There are females who need the avails of these labors for a livelihood; but not having been trained to them, they are not, of course, employed. Hence there is suffering in both ways. The sick suffer in the loss of the needed help, and the indigent woman suffers for want of the avails of that labor which she might have been trained to perform.

One great advantage of being able thus to obtain female attendants at a cheaper rate, is that the sick would be more likely to have the regular attention, or at least, the general care, of the same individual. Thousands and thousands of sick people have died, who might easily have recovered, had they been able to employ a regular nurse. Where a change of nurses takes place almost every day, no one of them feels that degree of responsibility which it is highly desirable that somebody, in this capacity, should feel.

5. I have spoken of the necessity of having young women trained to the art of taking care of the sick, that it may open a door to their sympathies. But it should also be done to open the door to their charities. Such charities as the gratuitous attendance of the sick, where it can be afforded, are among the most valuable which can possibly be bestowed. [Footnote: I mean, here, to speak only of those charities which go to *correct* the evils, which are in the world; for however great the good we may do in spending time and influence in correcting evil, the same amount of effort, rightly applied, must always do still more good in the way of prevention.] Had we ever so much money to give to the sick and distressed, it might be misapplied; or, at least, applied in a way we should not approve. Even if it were spent to procure good attendance, are we quite sure our own attendance would not be still more useful? Is it not always better to do the good ourselves—provided we are competent to do it—than by proxy; especially, by employing those whom we know little or nothing of? If we do all the good we are able to do, with our own hands, we feel that we have better discharged our duty, than if we had first turned our labor into money, and then applied the money to the same purpose.

But how is it possible, I shall doubtless be asked, that in a healthy community like that of our own New England, young women generally can be trained to understand this office?

There is no great difficulty in the case. Healthy as we are—that is, comparatively so—we have in every neighborhood, if not in every family, ample opportunities for initiating the young into this most indispensable art. It is not expected, nor is it indeed desirable, that they should be fully employed, or made fully responsible, at first. There should be a sort of apprenticeship served, to this trade as well as to any other. Indeed, I hardly know of an occupation or an art, which more demands a long apprenticeship, than this. Put, as I was going on to say, let young women, at a very early age, be gradually inducted into the office. Some young female of their own age, is perhaps sick. Let them solicit their mother and the friends of the diseased, to permit them to be present a part or all of the time, that they may observe and early understand the art of taking care of the sick.

Let the young woman *solicit* her mother, I say; because I apprehend, as I have done all along, that the work of reformation in this matter, no less than in others, must begin with the young woman. She finds herself twelve, fourteen or sixteen years of age, and entering upon a life involving duties and responsibilities, to her before unthought of—and for which she finds herself most sadly unprepared. She believes in the necessity of self-effort. What conscience tells her ought to be done, she decides to do. She goes forward intelligently and what she begins, she resolves, if possible, shall be finished.

Let it not be objected, that the introduction of the young to the sick room will expose them, unnecessarily, either to contagion or the breathing of bad air. For as to contagion, there is probably much less of it in the world than many suppose. But whether there is less or more danger, the best way to do, as the world is now situated, is, to inure ourselves, gradually, to disease. There are in New York and Philadelphia, many very aged persons, who have been employed as professional attendants of the sick during all the visitations of those cities with yellow fever and cholera, who have yet never taken either of those diseases.

It is our fear of taking disease, very often, which makes us take it. The sum total of the danger to the community, as a community, of contracting even contagious disease, will actually be much lessened, rather than increased, by all our young females being trained in the art and practice of nursing the sick. And the same might be said of the danger from bad air; because, the better the nurse is—that is, the more thoroughly and scientifically she understands her profession—the more pains will be taken in regard to ventilating, both the rooms of the sick and of those who are healthy.

I know, very well, that to be a complete professional nurse, requires a good deal of instruction in anatomy, physiology, hygiene and chemistry—to say nothing of botany, and pharmacy, and materia medica. But are not females fully competent to all this? Are they not as much so, to say the least, as males? Besides, the same information which is so indispensable to a nurse, if it should not be much wanted for this purpose, (for some females would not be needed as nurses, to a very great extent,) would be of inestimable value in the early management of a family.

What can be more pitiable, than to see a young widowed mother—say at twenty-five or thirty years of age—in poverty, in a situation remote from neighbors, with three or four children sick with some epidemic disease, while she is utterly unacquainted with the best methods of taking care of them. Let it be supposed, still further, that she is without a physician, and destitute of a nurse, excepting herself. What is she to do? Take care of them herself she cannot, as she may honestly tell you; having never taken care of a sick person, even a near relation, for so much as a single day or night in her whole life!

"I was sick and ye visited me," is represented, moreover, by the Judge of all the earth, as one of the grounds—not of salvation from sin—but of final reward in the world of spirits. But can any one believe our Saviour here means those empty, hollow-hearted visits now so common among us?—just going, I mean, to a sick neighbor's door, and asking how she does—or peradventure stepping in, only to stare at the sufferer, and with a half suppressed breath and a sigh, to hope to comfort her by wishing she may ultimately recover? No such thing. The Saviour, by visiting the sick, meant those kind and valuable offices which are worthy of the name; especially, when performed by the kind and gentle hand of a lovely, intelligent, benevolent and pious woman.

Oh, young woman! hadst thou but a glimpse of one half the angelic offices in thy power, how wouldst thou labor and pray for those qualities and that education, which would enable thee to act up to the dignity of thy nature, in the sight of God, angels and men! How wouldst thou labor to accomplish thy noble destiny.

CHAPTER XXX.

INTELLECTUAL IMPROVEMENT.

Futility of the question whether woman is or is not inferior to man. Conversation as a means of improvement. Taciturnity and loquacity. Seven rules in regard to conversation. Reading another means of mental progress. Thoughts on a perverted taste. Choosing the evil and refusing the good. Advice of parents, teachers, ministers, &c. Advice of a choice friend. Young people reluctant to be advised. Set hours for reading. Reading too much. Reading but a species of talking. Composition. Common mistakes about composing. Attempt to set the matter right. Journalizing. How a journal should be kept. Music. Vocal music something more than a mere accomplishment. Lectures and concerts. Studies. Keys of knowledge.

Much has been said, incidentally, in the preceding chapters, of the importance of extended intellectual improvement. Besides, I have treated at large on this subject in another volume, [Footnote: See the Young

Wife, chap. xxxiii. p. 292.] to which, as scarcely less adapted to the condition of young women than that of young wives, I must refer the reader. What I have to say in this work, will be little more than an introduction to the views there presented.

The long agitated question, whether woman is or is not equal to man in capacity for intellectual improvement, need not, surely, be discussed in this place. It is sufficient, perhaps, to know, that every young woman is capable of a much higher degree of improvement than she has yet attained, and to urge her forward to do all she can for herself, and to do it with all her might.

I have already mentioned, in preceding chapters, several sources of improvement—especially *observation* and *reflection*. But there are many sources of instruction accessible to those who are willing to be instructed; both external and internal. Some of these will now be made the subjects of a few passing remarks.

1. Conversation.—It is seldom, if ever, that we meet with an individual of either sex, whose conversational powers have been properly directed. To develope, cultivate and perfect these powers; seems hardly to be regarded as a part of education. We have left the tongue, like the rest of the frame to which it is attached, and of which it forms a component part, to go very much at random. In some, to be sure, it goes quite fast enough, and continues on the wing quite long enough; but it is too apt to go without rule, measure or profit—that is, comparatively so.

Now, to teach the tongue to go as it should—to teach it how to go, and how long, and when and where to make use of its power—is not, by any means, a small matter, or a very easy task. But ought not all this, and much more, to be done?

The old notion, that taciturnity is wisdom, is now very generally believed to be unfounded. These North American Indians who are most remarkable for this trait of character, are not found to be a whit wiser than other tribes who are more loquacious.

And what is found by observation to be true of nations or tribes, is equally true of individuals. One of the most taciturn persons I ever knew, and who passed with many for a very wise man, because he was very silent and grave, turned out, on a more intimate acquaintance, to be silent because he had nothing of importance to say.

Nor is loquacity uniformly a mark of wisdom. Some, indeed, talk a great deal, because they have a great deal to say: you will find a few such in a thousand. Others talk incessantly, either because they have nothing else to do, or will do nothing else. They do not, indeed, talk sense, or produce ideas; for sense and ideas they have not. At least, their sense is not common or sound sense: and as for their ideas, they are all superficial or borrowed.

Immense is the good which may be done in society, by conversation. There is hardly an art or a science, the *elements* of which, to say the least, may not be inculcated orally; that is, by conversation. But it is not necessary that our conversation, in order to be useful, should always be very scientific. There are a thousand topics of interest that have never yet been dignified with the name of science, which might yet be discussed in our familiar circles to a very great extent, and with both profit and pleasure.

When our conversation takes the form of story-telling, it is of still more absorbing interest, than when it is confined to mere ordinary colloquy. Here, again, a vast field of improvement opens upon our view. Few acquirements are more valuable to a young woman who expects ever to be at the head of a school or a family, than the art of relating a story well; and yet, owing to the neglect of this matter in education, no art, perhaps, is more uncommon.

A few leading principles, duly attended to, will, it is believed, enable those who have already had some teaching on this subject, to turn their conversation to better advantage; as well as aid, in the work of reformation, those who have not been duly instructed.

1. We should enunciate correctly, and speak distinctly. Few persons do this; and hence much of the pleasure which might otherwise be had, is lost.

2. We should endeavor, as far as in us lies, to speak with grammatical correctness. The custom of having two sorts of language—one for composition and the other for conversation—appears to me to have a very ill tendency. I would have no one converse in a language he does not understand; but I would have every one converse correctly.

3. We should endeavor to select such topics as are not only profitable to one party—either ourselves or those with whom we are conversing—but such also as are likely to be acceptable. It is of little use to *force a topic*, however great, in our judgment, may be its importance.

4. Conversation should be direct—though not confined too long to one point or topic. But while one subject is up, you should know how to keep it up; or if the thoughts of either party wander, you should know how to return to it, without too much apparent effort.

5. Conversation, like every thing else under the sun, should have its time and place. It is as wrong to converse when we ought to read, or study, or labor, or play, as it is to read or play when we ought to converse. Social life has a great many vacancies, as it were, which good, and sprightly, and well chosen conversation should fill up.

6. Conversation should be sprightly. If we converse not in this way, we might almost as well dispense with conversation entirely. We might nearly as well resort to the dead for society;—to the dead, I mean, who speak to us through the medium of their works. Of course I refer to conversation in general.

7. We should remember our responsibilities. "For every idle word that men speak, they shall give account thereof in the day of judgment"—said He who is to preside at the dread tribunal of which he spake: and an apostle has told us, that "our conversation should be in heaven;" that is, as I understand it, should be heavenly in its nature.

II. *Reading.*—There are, as I suppose, few young women of the present day, who do not read more or less; and to whom reading is not, in a greater or less degree, a source of intellectual improvement. Their reading is, however, governed chiefly by whim, or fancy, or accident—or at most, by taste. Some read newspapers only; some read only novels; some read every thing, and therefore nothing: Each of these methods—if methods they can be called—is wrong.

But shall not a young woman be governed by her taste? Is that to be turned wholly out of doors?

My reply is, that though our taste is not to be turned out of doors, wholly, it is, nevertheless, a very imperfect guide, and needs correction. Our intellect, like our moral and physical likes and dislikes, is, as I have elsewhere said, perverted by the fall. I will not say that our moral, intellectual and physical tastes are perverted in an equal degree; for I do not think so. Still there is a perversion, greater or less, of the whole man—in all his functions, faculties and affections. As a general rule, when left to our own course, we choose that food, for body, mind and soul, which, though it may be pleasant at first, is bitter afterwards. "There is a way which seemeth right unto a man, but the end thereof is death."

Still it may be said—If our intellectual tastes are perverted, how are they to be set right? Why not, I ask, in the same way that our moral taste is—by the word and truth of God? "To the law and to the testimony."

The application of the doctrines I am now advocating, belongs, most properly, to parents and teachers; religious teachers, especially. Parents, aided by ministers of the gospel, and perhaps the family physician, should decide for the young, individually, what means of intellectual improvement are best for them, all things considered; what books, society, studies, &c. But I must confine my remarks to books and reading.

It is not difficult to decide what the tastes of a child shall be, in regard to reading. I will not, indeed, say that a parent may at once do every thing she desires; but she may do a great deal. The child's moral and intellectual tastes are about as fully at her command, as its physical ones; and who shall say that her power to the latter respect, is second to any but that of the Creator?

It is not for parents, however, that I am now writing; but for those whose taste, by the aid or neglect of parents, is already formed. If formed on the basis of the word and truth of God—if they are inclined to prefer the best books and reject the worst—then all is well but if not, then the work of self-education is, in this respect, to set that right which has hitherto been wrong.

Hardly any thing can be of greater importance in this matter, than the assistance of a friend, in whom we can confide, in making our selection. This is as necessary in regard to newspapers, as to books. She who reads newspapers, indiscriminately, will derive little benefit from them; as her head will be filled with such a mixture of truth and falsehood, and wisdom and folly, as will be likely to do her more harm than good.

Few will read to advantage, who have not their set hours for reading. It is true, that unforeseen circumstances may, at times, break in upon our arrangement, and impede our progress in knowledge; but if we have no arrangement or system at all, we shall find our progress impeded still more.

Do not read too much. The world is almost deluged with books. Not only see that your selection is as it should be, in regard to the character of the books, but beware of having too many of them. A few, well read and understood, will be more valuable.

The importance of sometimes reading aloud, has been mentioned. It has other advantages, however, than merely the exercise of the lungs. With a proper monitor at hand, it may be made a useful aid in correcting our enunciation, as well as in improving our conversational powers. Reading is but speaking the thoughts of others instead of our own; and she is the best reader—and indeed most likely to be made wiser by reading—who speaks the most naturally. Our reading should be such, generally, that a friend in an adjoining room would find it difficult to tell whether we are reading or conversing.

III. *Composition.*—Next to conversation and reading, as a means of intellectual improvement, I place composition. This is nothing, either more or less—at least it should not be—than talking on paper. As reading is merely talking over the thoughts of others—conversing in another's words—so composition is merely conversing with others through the medium of a piece of paper.

It is a most delightful consideration, that it has pleased God to secure to us a written language. Are we grateful enough for the gift? Do we think enough of the privilege of conversing in this way with friends in every quarter of the globe?

One of the most valuable kinds of composition is letter-writing, or epistolary correspondence. This, above all, should be in the style of familiar though well directed conversation.

I wish, with all my heart, that people could get rid of the idea, that there should be one style for conversation, and another for writing. Here is the stumbling-stone on which youth of both sexes have been stumbling, time immemorial; and on which, I fear, many will be likely to stumble for some time to come.

Could they get rid of this strange belief—could they perceive, most clearly, that composition is nothing more than putting our thoughts on paper, instead of delivering them by word of mouth—and that conversation is nothing less than composition, except that the words are written as it were in the air, instead of being placed on a sheet of paper—how soon would the complaints about the tediousness of composition cease to be heard. Some young women, of sixteen, or eighteen, or twenty years of age, appear to regard letter-writing as childish. They talk of having once been so foolish as to be addicted to the practice; but as having now outgrown it. Such persons have no conception of the vast importance of this species of composition, as an aid to correct thinking and correct writing. The more we think, the more and better we are able to think; and the more we write, the more thoughts we have which we wish to put down.

One valuable form of putting down thoughts—next to letter-writing—consists in keeping a journal. I often wonder why our families and schools should encourage almost every thing else, rather than letter-writing and journalizing. Our familiar letters to familiar friends, might often consist of extracts from our daily journals.

But here, again, there has been great error. Journals have usually consisted of the driest details, or exteriors of events. The young should be encouraged to record their feelings in them; their hopes and fears—their anticipations and their regrets—their joys and their sorrows—their repentances and their resolutions. Such journals, with old and young, could not fail to advance the intellect, even if they should not improve the heart.

IV. *Music.*—Attention to music-vocal music, especially-should always form a part of female education. The day is gone by, as I trust, when it was customary to say that none but the *gifted* could acquire this accomplishment. It is now, I believe, pretty well understood, that all persons may learn to sing, as well as to read. Not, of course, equally well, in either case; but all can make a degree of progress.

I have called singing an accomplishment; but it seems to me to be much more. Its bearing upon the health, and even upon the intellect, is very great. Even its moral tendency is by no means to be overlooked.

The value of music, to soothe the feelings and cast out the evil spirits which haunt the path of human life, has never yet received that measure of attention which it deserves. Even in those parts of continental Europe, where all the peasants sing, and are accustomed to fill the air with their cheerful and harmonious voices as they go forth to prosecute their daily tasks, no less than in their families—even there, I say, the full power and value of music are not understood. They make it, by far too much, a sort of sensual gratification. Let it be redeemed, for a better and a nobler purpose. Let it become a companion of science and literature, as well as of industry and of virtue—and of religion, still more than all.

V. *Lectures and Concerts.*—Lectures are often useful, even when they do no more than afford an agreeable means of passing an hour's time. They are not indispensable to those young women who love study; but are more useful as a means of exciting inquiry in those who have very little fondness for it.

Besides, there are lectures, at times, on subjects which cannot be found in books; and in such cases they may be specially useful to all.

As for concerts, and parties of all sorts, attended as they usually are in the evening, there are many objections to them—though, as society is now regulated, it may not be best to denounce them altogether. Home is the proper place for young women, as well as for other honest people, after dark; at least this ought to be the general rule.

If lectures, concerts, &c., could be attended in the afternoon, there would be fewer objections to them. Even then, however, there would probably be more or less of intellectual dissipation connected with their attendance. It is to be regretted that time, which is so valuable, cannot be better employed, than in mere running abroad, because others are going.

VI. *Studies.*—If the young woman could have some judicious friend, male or female, to advise her what books to read, and what studies to pursue—and if the non-essentials in dress, &c., were discarded—I cannot help thinking that life is long enough, to give her an opportunity to become mistress of every thing which is usually thought to belong to a good English education. I will venture to say, that there is hardly a girl of twelve years of age, whose circumstances are so unfavorable, as to prevent her from thus acquiring the keys of knowledge by the time she is twenty-five years of age, could she be directed in a proper manner.

I have spoken of acquiring the *keys* of knowledge, as if this were the first object of a course of studies. And such I regard it. I know, indeed, that we reap some of the fruits of almost all our acquired knowledge, immediately: still, the greater part remains for years to come.

No young woman should fail to be thoroughly versed in spelling, reading, writing, composition, grammar, geography and arithmetic—and as much as possible, in anatomy, physiology, hygiene, chemistry, botany, natural history, philosophy, domestic and political economy, civil and ecclesiastical history, biography, and the philosophy of the Bible—to say nothing of geology, and the higher branches of mathematics.

One word more in regard to your handwriting. Nothing is more common, in these days, than to write in a most illegible manner—a mere scribble. Now, whatever young men may do in this respect, I beseech every young woman to avoid this wretched, slovenly habit. Hardly any thing appears more interesting to me, in a young woman, than a neat, delicate, and at the same time plain style of hand-writing.

Do not pursue too many studies at once: it is the most useless thing that can be done. Your knowledge, should you get any, would in that way be confused and indefinite, instead of being clear, and practical, and useful to you. I would never pursue more than one or two leading sciences at one time; and in general, I think that one is better than more. If you pursue more than one, let them be such as are related; as geography and history.

Let me say, in closing this chapter, that the great end of all intellectual culture, is to teach the art of *thinking*, and of *thinking right*. To learn to think, merely, is to rise only one degree above the brute creation. To learn to think *well*, however, is noble; worthy of the dignity of human nature, and of the Author of that nature.

CHAPTER XXXI.

SOCIAL IMPROVEMENT.

Improvement in a solitary state. The social relations. Mother and daughter. Father and daughter. Brother and sister. The elder sister. Brethren and sisters of the great human family. The family constitution. Character of Fidelia. Her resolutions of celibacy. In what cases the latter is a duty. A new and interesting relation. Selection with reference to it. Principles by which to be governed in making a selection. Evils of a hasty or ill-judged selection. Counsellors. Anecdote of an unwise one. Great caution to be observed. Direction to be sought at the throne of grace.

Were there but a single individual in the wide world, that individual, with the laws that woman now has to guide her—laws internal and external, natural and revealed—would be susceptible of endless and illimitable improvement. She might make advances every day—and it would he her duty to do so— upward toward the throne of God, and towards the perfection of him who occupies it.

But if much might be done by an individual in a solitary state, how much more may be accomplished in the social state in which it has pleased our Heavenly Father to place us? It is difficult to turn our eyes in any direction, without being met by numerous and striking proofs of divine wisdom and benevolence; but if there be any one thing in the whole moral world, short of the redemption by Jesus Christ, which overwhelms me with wonder, and leads me to adore more than any thing else, it is the divine wisdom and benevolence, as manifested in the social state allotted to man.

How interesting—how exceedingly so—the relation between a mother and a daughter? And how many blessings—deficient as many mothers are in knowledge and love—are showered upon the head of a young woman, through maternal instrumentality! In no case; however, is this relation more interesting, than when the young woman is just beginning to act for herself. Then, if ever, should she avail herself of them. She knows little of the world before her—either of the dangers on the one hand, or the advantages on the other. Of these, however, the mother knows much. Let the daughter value her society and good counsel above all else human, and lay hold of it as for her life.

How interesting, too, the relation between a wise and good father, and a virtuous and affectionate daughter! I am most struck, however, with this relation—and most reminded of the divine goodness in its institution—when I see a daughter ministering to the wants, moral and physical, of a very aged relative, parent or grandparent; one who is superannuated or sick.

There are, in civilized society—and above all, where the rays of the blessed gospel of the Son of God have been let in—scenes on which angels themselves might delight to gaze, and on which I have no doubt they do gaze with the most intense delight. Would that such scenes were still more frequent! Would that filial love was always what it should be, instead of degenerating into cold formalities.

"How have I been charmed;" says Addison, "to see one of the most beauteous women the age has produced, kneeling to put on an old man's slipper." And so have I. It is a sight which revives one's hopes of fallen nature. No matter if the infirmities of the parent are the consequences of his own folly, vice and crime, the same soft hand is still employed, day after day—and the same countenance is lighted up with a smile, at being able thus to employ it.

But when to the tenderest love on the part of a young woman in this relation, and to the kindest efforts to promote the temporal happiness and comfort of those whom she holds dear is joined a love for the mind and soul; when every opportunity, is laid hold of with eagerness, to inform, and improve, and elevate—and this, too, though the subject of her labor is the most miserable wreck of humanity of which we can conceive; when to works of love are added the warmest prayers, at the bedside and elsewhere, for Almighty aid and favor; the interest of the scene is indescribable. It needs a more than mortal pen or pencil to portray it.

There are other relations of society—relations of the young woman, I mean, in particular—which are of great importance and interest. Among these, are the relations of brother and sister.

Perhaps I am inclined to make too much of the passage of Scripture—already noticed in another chapter—where Cain is said to have been set over Abel, in the very language which is used to signify the superiority of Adam over Eve. And yet it must mean something. There is a mutual dependence between brothers and sisters of every age, which should result in continual improvement—intellectual, moral and religious. The duties involved in this relation, however, will be more especially binding on elder brothers and sisters; and as it appears to me, above all, on elder sisters. Indeed, in this respect, it is impossible for me to be mistaken. An elder sister is a sort of second mother; and she often fulfils the place of a mother. Oh, how important-how sacred—the trust committed to her keeping.

I have seen the care of a large family devolve, by the death of the mother, upon the elder daughter. Instead of her being disheartened at all, I have known her to go forward in the pathway of duty—sensible, at the same time, of her dependence on her Heavenly Father—and not only instruct the other children, but "train them up," in same good degree, "in the way they should go."

Do you think I respected or loved this young woman the less, because she was thus early a house—keeper, a matron, and a mother? Do you think I esteemed her the less, because—exclusive of the common school—she had no seminary of instruction? Her education was a thousand times more valuable than that of the fashionable routine of the schools, without the kind of discipline she had. A world whose females were all educated in the family schools—and especially in the school of affliction, and poverty, and hardship—would be incomparably a better world than one whose young women should "wear soft clothing," and live in "kings' courts"—who should be educated by merely fashionable mothers, amid ease and abundance, and "finished" at the institute or the boarding school.

Let me not be understood, in all this, as undervaluing kind mothers, and boarding schools, and comforts—and luxuries, even—in themselves considered. All I mean to discourage, is, a reliance on them, to the exclusion of other things of more importance. If we could have the latter in the first place—difficulties, hard-ships, hard labor, and adversity—and upon these engraft the former, I should like it exceedingly well. What I dislike is, not ornament, in itself, but ornament on that which is not worth ornamenting; and above all, *nothing but ornament.*

Let every young woman whose eye meets these paragraphs, rejoice, if she has younger brothers or sisters—or even if she has brothers or sisters at all. The younger may do something for the older, as well as the older much for the younger. And if she is without either, there are probably other and remoter relatives for whom something may be done.

I have alluded, elsewhere, to grand-parents There are usually uncles, aunts and cousin's—sometimes in great numbers. There is much due to these. I know, very well, that out over-refinement, in an over-refined and diseased society, says otherwise, of late; and that our time is expended more and more—especially that of females—on our own dear selves to the exclusion of remoter relatives. But this should not be the case. Whether we have brethren or sisters, properly so called, together with other more distant relatives, or not, *we have brethren and sisters.* The world is but a great family; and all are brethren, or ought to be so. We should love all—even our enemies—as brethren; but we should love, with the deepest and most enduring affection, those who love God most ardently. "My mother and brethren are they that hear the word of God and do it," said the Saviour; and it is only in proportion as we possess his spirit, that we shall be found to belong, in the truest sense, to his family.

The ties of which I have been speaking, in the preceding paragraphs, will have but poorly answered their purpose, if they have not had the effect to raise us to this universal love referred to by the Saviour. For this they were chiefly instituted; and to this, in the best state of human society, do they tend. They do not lead us to love relations, usually so called, any less: neither did they have this effect on Jesus. But they lead us to love the world at large, more.

If young women would have the spirit of our Lord and Saviour—or if they would be instruments in his hands of hastening the glad day of his more complete reign on the earth and in the hearts of his intelligent family—they must strive to come up to this love of the human family. It is to elevate them to this love, I again say, that the family institution, with all the interesting relations which grow out of it, was instituted. When it has accomplished this work, though it will not cease to be valuable, in the abstract, it will be less valuable relatively—because it will absorb a smaller proportion of our thoughts and affections, and leave a larger proportion for the world in general, and its Creator.

I have quoted, elsewhere, the sentiments of Addison, in regard to the filial affection of daughters. In the same paper, this interesting writer embodies his views on this subject, in the character of a young woman by the name of Fidelia, whose devotion to her father he describes as follows:

"Fidelia is now in the twenty-third year of her age; but the application of many admirers, and her quick sense of all that is truly elegant and noble in the enjoyment of a plentiful fortune, are not able to draw her from the side of her good old father. When she was asked by a friend of her deceased mother to admit the courtship of her son, she answered that she had a great respect and gratitude to her for the overture in behalf of one so near to her; but that during her father's life, she would admit into her heart no value for any thing which should interfere with her endeavors to make his remains of life as happy and easy as could be expected in his circumstances. The happy father has her declaration that she will not marry during his life, and the pleasure of seeing that resolution not uneasy to her."

Now, though I am not quite satisfied with the selfishness of the father, in this case—nor with the notion of Fidelia, that the particular friendship of another would interfere materially with her filial duties—yet I do not undertake to say that there are no cases in which a young woman has the right—the moral right—to make resolutions not unlike that made by Fidelia. It does not seem that her resolution to neglect the society of others for the sake of discharging an important filial duty, was for a longer period, than during the short life of a very decrepid old father.

I have introduced this subject in this place, as the preface to a series of remarks on that particular relation which every young woman—except, perhaps, a few who are situated like Fidelia—ought to be prepared to sustain, and to sustain well. Indeed, I consider this to be paramount, at a suitable age, to every other; and that no duty can, as a general rule, be more obligatory.

He who instituted the law of marriage, has not, indeed, condescended to say how early or in what circumstances this command must be yielded to, or obeyed; but, as a general rule, he requires it to be obeyed, in some form or other, and at some time or other. Or, to express the views I entertain more correctly, I should say, that no young woman, in ordinary circumstances, has a right to resolve to neglect the subject forever—or to say she never will marry. She is to consider the command of the Creator as obligatory, as a general fact, on the whole human race. She must remember, moreover, that if it is binding on the whole, it must be so on the individuals composing that whole.

On these principles the education of every young woman should, as I think, be conducted; and if, by the neglect of parents, masters or guardians, it has not been so, then it should be the aim of the young woman herself, in her efforts at self-education, to supply what has been by others omitted. Some of the items in this work of education have been alluded to—not only in the chapter on "Domestic Concerns;" and in that on "Economy," but elsewhere. My purpose at the present time, is merely to speak of the selection of her society with reference to her future state of life.

This is a subject of the highest importance to the happiness—present and future—of every young woman. The marriage relation, considered only as a means of completing the education of the parties, is one of immense importance. But it is of still greater importance, in reference to other duties which it involves. Hence it requires much forethought and reflection. Let me prevail with you, therefore, when I urge upon you the following considerations:

1. Never think for one moment of the society of any other than a good man. Whatever may be his extrinsic endowments—wit, beauty, talent, rank, property or prospects—all should be as nothing to you, unless his character is what it should be. Of course, I am not encouraging you to look for angelic perfection or purity on this earth; but do not make too many allowances, on the other hand, for frailty. A close examination, as with the microscope, will disclose irregularity and roughness on the most polished or smooth surface: how then will that surface appear which is uneven without the microscope? If it were possible for your associate for life to come apparently near celestial purity and excellence, a closer acquaintance would, most undoubtedly, convince you that he was of terrestrial origin. Do the best you can, therefore, and you will do ill enough.

2. It is not sufficient, however, that the friend you seek should be good—that is, negatively so: he must do good. Multitudes, in these days, pass for good men because they do no harm; or because, at most, they maintain a good standing, and are benevolent in the eye of the world. I know of more than one person in the world, who gives his property by thousands, annually—and whose praise is in all the churches—who never yet gave any thing worth naming, in his life, if the gospel rule on this subject is the correct one— that the widow who *of her penury* cast into the treasury two mites, in reality cast in more than all they who of *their abundance* bestowed large and liberal sums.

Let your associate, therefore, be a doer of good, in deed and in truth. This is said, however, with the supposition that you are so yourself; for if I have not already convinced you that the great end for which you were sent into the world is to do good, I shall not expect to do so by any remarks which could be thrown in here. If you are still out of the way, it is to be feared you will remain so: nor shall I expect you—for reasons to be seen presently—to seek the society of those who do not possess the same turn of mind.

3. It is highly desirable that the individual with whom you associate for life, should be something more than merely a good man. This, however, does not explain my meaning. For are there not many of the most excellent persons in the world, whom you would not willingly take for a daily companion? Do you not desire likeness in opinion, taste, purpose, &c.? Might not the two very best persons in the world be unhappy in each other's constant society, if they were exceedingly unlike each other?

In the establishment, then, of this interesting relation, seek by all means an individual who appears to entertain views of social life, as much as possible, like your own. Does he find his happiness in going abroad, or in lounging? Is he impatient in the society of children? Is he a great friend of parade and excitement? And are you the reverse of all this? Do you love most the quiet and retirement of home—and to be surrounded by infancy and childhood? Do you dread, above almost all things in the world, excitement and parade?

Does your friend hate nothing so much as his own thoughts and reflections? Does he dread, also, like the cholera or the plague, all efforts at mental or moral improvement? Does he hate improving conversation—and above all, those books and associates which have the improvement and elevation of the body and spirit, for their great and leading object? And have you a different taste—entirely so? Do you live—do you eat, drink, sleep, wake, exercise, dress, labor, play, converse, read, and think, and pray that you may become wiser, and better, and holier?

In short, is the ultimate object of the one, the gratification of self; and does all, with him, terminate in the external; while the other seeks primarily, in all things, the improvement, the holiness and the happiness of herself and others? How can such persons be suitable companions for each other? Can two walk together, says the Scripture, unless they are agreed—that is, agreed as to the main points and purposes of life?

I know of no being whom I so much pity, as a young woman who, believing, perhaps, that a "reformed rake," once handsome, or it may be, a wit, makes the best companion, becomes chained for life to a stupid, shiftless creature—one whose energies of body and soul are exhausted, and seem unsusceptible of being renovated or restored—one, too, with whom, in that more intimate acquaintance which time and circumstances afford her, proves to be totally unworthy of her hand or her heart!

I have said that I know of no being so pitiable, as a young woman thus situated. I know of none, I mean to say, except a young man in similar circumstances. Did the effects of these unhappy companionships terminate on themselves, the misfortune would not be so great. Woman, at any rate, with her fortitude, might endure it. But it is not usually so; and here is the great evil. Misery is inflicted on a new generation; one that has done nothing to deserve it.

Let me entreat my readers, therefore, while I urge them to regard the companionship of which I am now speaking as a matter of duty, to be exceedingly careful in their selection of a companion. Choose; but do not be in haste. On the wisdom of your choice, much more depends than you can now possibly imagine:—it is for your life. Would you could realize this truth: for though so old and so often repeated that it may appear rather stale, it is not the less true for its age.

Have nothing to do, above all, with those who despise your sex. There is a large number of young men— much larger, indeed, than you may be aware, who have caught the spirit, not to say sentiments, of Byron, in regard to woman.

They have *caught* them, I say; but this, perhaps, is not so. I will only say they *have* them. I know not how, as a general fact, they came by them. I can only say that they are often very early imbibed; and that they grow with their growth, and strengthen with their strength. Would to Heaven this utter skepticism in regard to female worth and purity could be removed; or rather prevented. It is the bane of social life—as I could show, were I disposed to do so, by a thousand illustrations.

As a general rule—to which, perhaps, there are some exceptions—it is according to human nature to suspect others to be wanting in those virtues which we are conscious we are wanting in ourselves. Find a person wanting in sterling integrity, and he is the very person to be found complaining of the want of it in others. I will not say that his complaints are not sometimes—indeed, quite too often—just; I only say, that whether just or not, neither his suspicions nor complaints prove them to be so.

Beware, then—I beseech you, beware—of the young man who is ever prating about the innate worthlessness, not to say vice, of your sex. I do not say, reject him forever, simply on suspicion; for that would be to go to the other extreme. But though I have admitted that there may possibly be exceptions in regard to the general rule I have laid down, I also insist that they are rare. Therefore, I again say, be wary in forming your friendships—and especially so, in suffering them to become more and more intimate.

Precisely in these circumstances is it, that you may derive immense benefit from a discreet female friend. But in this, too, you must be deliberate, and use great judgment; for there are many whose views on this subject are such as entirely to disqualify them for the office of an adviser. I remember hearing a lady of great gravity—though of much good sense in all other respects—say, that she thought the friends of a young woman were much more competent to select a companion for her, than she was to make the selection for herself. I was so struck with the remark, that not knowing but I misapprehended her meaning, I ventured to inquire whether she really meant to say, that other people could judge better in regard to selecting a companion for life, than the parties most concerned in the choice. To which she answered, Yes, without hesitation; and immediately went upon a defence of her opinion. I was as little pleased, however, with the defence, as with the assertion; for the whole thing carried absurdity on the very face of it. It cannot, surely, be so; it is contrary to the very nature of things.

I cannot help counselling you to be as wary of such an adviser, as of the friend to whom she would direct your attention. The choice—the final choice—be it never forgotten, rests on you: because on you rests the responsibilities. While, therefore, you seek, with great earnestness, for advice, seek it as advice only. Neither seek, nor admit, in any case, a dictator.

Be it also ever remembered, that it is your duty to sift, with great care, the opinions and views of one in whom you are daily becoming more and more deeply interested. If it be even true, that woman is *not* distinguished for perseverance, let this fact only stimulate you to use what powers of perseverance you possess. Though you are not to be held responsible for the exercise of talents which you have not, you *are* to account for what talents you have; and fearful may be the reward of the individual who is found delinquent in the matter before us; fearful in this life, even were it possible to escape punishment in the life to come. Let a comparison, then, be faithfully made of your views on all important subjects:—as female superiority or inferiority; selfishness and benevolence; dress and equipage; education of ourselves and others; discipline—its means, instruments and ends; household management; amassing property; the chief end of human existence; particular duties, &c.

While I would encourage every young woman to look forward to married life as a matter of duty, I am very far from desiring to encourage that indiscriminate conversation, which, among young women, is rather common. Let it be discussed by the young, chiefly in the company of their parents. Above all, let not females be found talking with great interest on this subject in the presence of the other sex. Such conversation, in such circumstances, is evil, and only evil, in its tendency.

Parents may prevent this mistake in young women, if they will. The mother, at least, can prevent it. Where mothers manage the matter as it ought to be managed, you will not find daughters, on going into company, so deeply interested in these matters that nothing seems so to loosen the tongue, light up the countenance, and brighten the eye, as conversation about the latest engagements and marriages, and nothing so much or so quickly interest them in a newspaper, even a religious one, and that, too, on the Sabbath, as the list of marriages. Alas! do mothers or daughters know what are the practical common sense inferences from this conduct, where it greatly abounds.

Remember, moreover, in this matter, as well as in all other matters which concern your own happiness and the happiness of others—in this matter, I might say, which concerns your happiness more than almost all others—to seek the direction of that Being who has said, "If any lack wisdom, let him ask of God." You cannot, surely, obey this first injunction on the human race, without first and always, at every step of your course, seeking for his approbation. You cannot, in one word, be concerned in a duty which may involve the destinies—present and eternal—of millions and millions of human beings, without looking upward toward the throne of God, and soliciting, with all the humility, as well as confidence, of the most devoted child of an earthly parent, that wisdom and guidance which are to be found in all fulness in the Father of lights, and which, when properly apprehended, can never mislead you.

CHAPTER XXXII.

MORAL PROGRESS.

Importance of progress. Physical improvement a means rather than an end. The same true of intellectual improvement. The general homage which is paid to inoffensiveness. Picture of a modern Christian family. Measuring ourselves by others. Our Saviour the only true standard of comparison. Importance of self-denial and self-sacrifice. Blessedness of communicating. Young women urged to emancipate themselves from the bondage of fashion, and custom, and selfishness.

After all I have said of the importance of physical, intellectual and social improvement and progress, it is *moral* progress for which we were, pre-eminently, created. The great end of Christianity itself—to use the words of a learned and eloquent divine—is, to make men better than they were before: but whether or not this expresses the entire truth, one thing is certain—that wherever Christianity fails to make man better, it fails of accomplishing its whole intention respecting him. Perhaps the apostle expressed the idea I would inculcate, in the fewest words and in the clearest manner, when he required his converts to "grow in grace, and in the knowledge of our Lord and Saviour Jesus Christ."

Mere physical improvement—or even physical perfection, were it attainable—would hardly be worth the pains, if it were any thing more than a means to an end. We might study the subject of health, and practice its excellent rules with the utmost zeal and faithful conscientiousness; and yet it would hardly prove a blessing to us, if it only gave us the more efficiency in the service of the world, the flesh and the devil. And the same, or nearly the same, may be said of intellectual improvement and progress. Though the general tendency of both—when conscience is properly trained and the heart set right—is beneficial, yet it is not necessarily so, without a right heart and correct conscience. Satan is not wanting—so to speak— in intelligence or physical energy.

Physical and intellectual development and progress, therefore, are little more than means to secure an end. If they prove to be what it was the original intention of the Creator they should be, they are eminently conducive to our highest interests, both as respects this world and the world which is to come. If otherwise, they do but accelerate, and in the end aggravate, our doom. They tend but to make our condemnation the more sure, and the more dreadful.

I have urged, elsewhere, the importance of conscientiousness in every thing we do: let me especially recommend you to make continual progress in excellence or holiness, a matter of conscience. Do not be continually measuring yourself—above all, your spiritual self—by your neighbors. If you are the true disciple of Christ, and if you are what a Christian should be in this land of Christianity, you will not indulge yourself in comparisons with any but the Saviour himself. You will be daily and hourly striving to possess more and more of his spirit; in the belief that without the spirit of Christ, you neither are nor can be his.

It is painful to think of the great number of individuals who go through life—often through a long life—and yet accomplish so little for themselves and others. That they are free from outward immorality or blame—as much so at least as their neighbors—seems to satisfy them. Some of the best families I know, are trained in this way. They are excellent people; they are disciples of Christ, if there are any such in the world: we cannot say aught against them, if we would. They seem to discharge all the external duties of our holy religion with a most scrupulous exactness; and they seem—the whole family—to bear the image of Christ. Whatever is true or lovely, is theirs; or appears to be so.

And yet, if you examine closely the matter, you will find that much of all this is the result of circumstances. They possess, by inheritance, a happy temper—or they are in circumstances which make virtue easy to them.

But the spirit and genius of Christianity require a great deal more than mere inoffensiveness—though that is, of itself, certainly, a great deal. They require continual progress from glory to glory. But this progress can only be made amid self-denial and cross-taking. "Whoso taketh not up his cross," daily and hourly, is not a true disciple of the great Teacher. It is even through "much tribulation" only, that we can enter into the kingdom of our Lord and Saviour.

Now, to what self-denials, what tribulations, what taking up of the cross, do these easy, lovely families of which I am speaking, ever subject themselves? Trained happily, they are generally healthy—and therefore they have few trials from sickness. They live in the midst of abundance, and always have done so—abundance of food, clothing, &c., and of what they regard as of the best quality. They have more than heart can wish: their eyes, as it were, stand out with fatness. They know nothing of want: they know nothing even of inconvenience—except for some hapless moment, when a neighbor gets a little ahead of them in the fashion of their dress, their equipage, or their tables. Then a feeling of envy—peradventure a half expressed feeling of detraction—appears to mar, for a short time, their peace.

I have said that these inoffensive people—these do-no-harm Christians—know nothing of want. When and where have they cut themselves short of any thing to which they were lawfully entitled, for the sake of doing good to others? They have, indeed, performed works of charity and mercy, as much as other people of their own property and standing in society. But they have given, always, of their abundance. They have never so given as to impoverish the giver—so as to make themselves feel the least privation. They have visited the sick: but when has the time they have given, seriously incommoded them? Have they not had time enough left for their own purposes? Have they not, in this respect, given of their abundance? Perhaps they have clothed the poor, to some extent; but have they denied themselves to do it? Have not their closets, and houses, and the neighboring livery stable, been well furnished and supplied, notwithstanding? Have they not given, in this respect, wholly of their abundance—and not, like the good woman mentioned in the gospel, of their penury?

It is exceedingly painful, I say again, to find professedly good people among us living, as Watts calls it, at such a poor, dying rate; the professed disciples of a Master who became poor for their sakes, by giving up, not only the luxuries of life, but even many of its necessaries—and yet not giving up or denying themselves a single thing all their lives long.

Can such people expect to make advances in holiness—to grow in grace and in the knowledge of Christ—and yet not act like him, or follow him? For be it always remembered—the benefits of doing good are to those *who do it, more than to those to whom it is done*. This is the ordination and arrangement of Providence. "It is more blessed to give than to receive." How sad a mistake, then, is made by those who seem—from their conduct—to think there is little happiness in giving; and that their charities abridge, by so much, their happiness, instead of adding to it.

Young woman, should it be your lot to belong to one of these happy and excellent families—for I do not deny that they are among our best people, after all, though they are very far from having, as yet, come up to the self-denying, self-sacrificing spirit of the Lord that bought them, and become willing to be poor, and to suffer not a little want of time, money, &c. for even their own apparent necessities, temporal or spiritual—I say, if in the providence of God, you have been accustomed to see almost the whole time and labor of a family, with the avails of a handsome, or at least respectable property, used up year after year by that family, in eating, and drinking, and sleeping, and dressing *comfortably*—in mere passive enjoyment, in one word—while the blessedness of active enjoyment, in the doing of good to others, has been hardly known—be it yours to break the chain that binds this circle of selfishness, and go forth to the work of impoverishing yourself, as did your Lord and Master. Think not to make any considerable moral progress, otherwise! The soul must have food, as well as the body. This continual indulgence of the body, while the soul is unfed, or only fed just enough to keep it from starving, will never do for you. If you yield to the influence of this fashionable kind of excellence, and strive not to rise higher, I will not say that you will live to little purpose; but I will say, that you will have but very little of real, valuable, immortal life, till you pass beyond the bounds of time and space. Whereas, you ought to begin your heaven here. For "this is the will of God, even your sanctification;" and it was the prayer of Paul concerning some to whom he wrote—"The God of peace sanctify you wholly."

Will you not, then, O young woman! in view of these considerations, seek for deliverance from the spell that binds thousands and millions of otherwise good people to a narrow, selfish circle, in which they continually wander—coming round and round again, every night, to the same spot, or nearly the same, but making no considerable progress? Will you not study, and labor, and pray, for more and more of the spirit of Him, who not only stripped himself of every glory to which he, had been accustomed, but, instead of retaining that which was his divine right, deprived himself of every thing which is calculated to make life comfortable in the common sense of the term, and only sought his happiness in perfecting holiness in the fear of God, by living and dying for his brethren—the whole human family? Will you not henceforth study to be more and more conformed to the Divine image—and to act less and less in conformity with a world whose predominating motive to action, is selfishness?